A MAN WHO LOVED THE STARS

Clarke L. Gage,
1994

John Brashear. Portrait by J. W. Vale.
Allegheny Observatory

A MAN
WHO LOVED
THE STARS

The Autobiography of
John A. Brashear

UNIVERSITY OF PITTSBURGH PRESS

Published by the University of Pittsburgh Press, Pittsburgh, Pa., 15260

Feffer and Simons, Inc., London

Manufactured in the United States of America

Library of Congress Cataloging-in-Publication Data

Brashear, John A. (John Alfred), 1840–1920.
    [John A. Brashear]
    A man who loved the stars: the autobiography of John A. Brashear.
        p.   cm.
    Originally published: John A. Brashear. New York : American Society of
Mechanical Engineers, 1924. With new introd.
    "This edition omits chapter 19, Brashear's account of his trip to the Orient
in 1916, and chapter 20, a group of letters selected by the editor"—Introd.
    Includes Index.
    ISBN 0-8229-1151-5.   ISBN 0-8229-6089-3 (pbk.)
    1. Brashear, John A. (John Alfred). 1840–1920.   2. Astronomical
instruments—Design and construction—History.   3. Astronomers—
United States—Biography.   4. Engineers—United States—
Biography.
I. Title.
QB36.B85A3 1988
522'.2'0924—dc19
[B]   87–25190
                                                  CIP

Grateful acknowledgment is made to the Brashear
Association for permission to reproduce photographs
from their collection.

CONTENTS

INTRODUCTION

With this edition the University of Pittsburgh Press reissues the autobiography of one of Pittsburgh's most illustrious citizens, John A. Brashear. Working almost entirely on his own and without the benefit of a formal education, Brashear made a significant contribution to the development of technology. His personality must have been magnetic and his ability to communicate his dreams equally engaging, for as his fame grew, he was befriended by such wealthy, powerful, and highly demanding Pittsburgh philanthropists as William Thaw and Andrew Carnegie. These men increasingly made a point of injecting Brashear into positions of influence over the cultural and educational life of the Pittsburgh community. In this brief and modest memoir, historians of science and technology will find a fascinating case history of significant technological advance and its relation to the science of its day. Filled with intriguing observations of late nineteenth century steel-mill technology, the state of Pittsburgh neighborhoods, and the functioning of various church, educational, and civic groups, this book should also delight social and Western Pennsylvania historians, both professional and amateur.

John Brashear's technological achievement was to revolutionize the grinding of optical lenses. Although he was largely oblivious to the significance of the basic science which was elucidated by measurements with his instruments, he had a profound effect on the development of both physics and astronomy. During the past twenty years, historians of science have frequently discussed the symbiotic relationship between science and technology, each of whose advances normally proceed from the recent successes of the other. Brashear's autobiography sets forth the attitudes of a very articulate technologist as he advances his field and learns that pure scientists, in whose research he has little interest and less knowledge, are quite anxious to work with him.

Brashear's skill and perfectionism in grinding glass to better tolerance than others could were of enormous value to optical spectroscopy—the study of the wavelength (color) distribution of the light emitted or absorbed by a material. In the first two decades of the twentieth century, spectroscopy provided the most powerful single tool for unraveling the mysteries of the atom. During the nineteenth century, spectroscopists had analyzed the light emitted and absorbed by a wide variety of atoms and molecules, cataloging for each species the characteristic wavelengths of this light. This in itself had produced a revolution in chemical analysis, profoundly affecting the science and technology of the day and exciting the popular imagination. It was to the popular interest in this new technology that Arthur Conan Doyle appealed when he had Sherlock Holmes use chemical analysis to test samples of cloth, tobacco, and other clues. The neon light also dates from this period.

The origin of the observed wavelength distribution was not understood until about 1910 when Niels Bohr explained the wavelengths observed for the hydrogen atom in terms of a planetary atomic model with a negatively charged electron orbiting a positively charged proton. In Bohr's model a burst of light (called a photon) emitted by the atom must carry away exactly the right amount of energy to take the atom from the definite allowed energy of its initial orbit to the definite energy of its final orbit. The energy of such a photon is specified completely by its wavelength. Thus the only wavelengths which the spectroscopists should see are those which permit one allowed state of the atom to transform into another: conversely, the scientist can infer ever finer details about the allowed energy states of the atom by measuring more closely the wavelengths of the photons emitted by the atom. From Bohr's time on, spectroscopists struggled to resolve finer and finer details of wavelength distributions in the hope of answering the ever-more-complex questions posed by the rapidly evolving quantum theory of atoms and molecules.

The need for increasingly finer resolution of detail sorely taxed the optical technology of the day. Brashear, with his great skill, and his willingness to accept orders for devices on which he was guaranteed to lose money, supplied the crucial technology at just the time it was needed. Unassuming, and unaware of the scientific significance of his lenses, he was genuinely puzzled at the royal reception he received as he toured the spectroscopy laboratories of Europe, each of which clearly hoped to compete in the next round of experiments by acquiring the best possible optical equipment from Brashear's workshop.

Brashear's impact on astronomy was more obvious to him both because of his strong amateur interest in astronomy and because the contributions of observations made with his telescopes were more accessible to lay understanding. The common theme in his relations with

astronomical observatories all over the world was his reputation for never shipping a device that failed to meet
specifications. Others at the time, and lamentably, in our
own, frequently shipped inferior devices rather than take a
financial loss. Brashear's unique combination of technical
virtuosity and unworldly lack of concern with profits was
detected by Professor Samuel P. Langley of the University
of Pittsburgh's Allegheny Observatory, and he alerted
William Thaw to Brashear's promise. With financial help
and business guidance from Thaw, Brashear filled orders
for high quality lenses at many of the world's best observatories. The 30-inch Keeler reflecting telescope at the
Allegheny Observatory was a state-of-the-art marvel in its
day. Using it, Professor Frank Schlesinger showed in 1920
that stars other than the sun also rotate. Another of
Brashear's most successful telescopes was the workhorse
72-inch reflector at the Dominion Astrophysical Observatory in Vancouver.

As Brashear's technical successes brought him increasingly to the attention of wealthy benefactors, his winning
personality induced them to provide him ever more financial support and to involve him in their other cultural
projects. Like many self-taught men, including his benefactor Carnegie, Brashear had a profound respect for education. He served two years as acting chancellor of the
University of Pittsburgh and then became a member of the
committee which established the Carnegie Institute of
Technology (today known as Carnegie-Mellon University).
Brashear was also chosen by Henry Clay Frick to admin-
ister a trust dedicated to improving teaching in the
Pittsburgh public schools. His involvement with education

in Pittsburgh at all levels is one of several themes in this work which provide insight into the social, cultural, and industrial development of Western Pennsylvania.

Brashear's account shows that scientific research funding, general philanthropy, and the mechanics of running a small business were all significantly different a hundred years ago. To secure funding, modern scientists must present their ideas clearly in writing to be evaluated by a committee of their peers; this is partly because research is so much more expensive and partly because the government (which now provides most research funds) and charitable foundations want to be sure they are supporting the best possible work. Brashear's work was so good and his ability to communicate, as shown in this autobiography, so impressive that he would almost certainly have been supported if the present system had been the norm in his day. On the other hand, one wonders how many gifted scientists of his day were unable to develop their ideas because their temperaments were poorly matched to the somewhat capricious system of personalized philanthropy.

No small business of yesterday or today could hope to survive with pricing policies like Brashear's. The note from Thaw of 1885 (page 93) is both amusing and revealing as Thaw—director of the Pennsylvania Railroad—tells Brashear that he cannot afford to sell his final product for only a little more than the cost of the initial raw piece of glass. Brashear's firm could not possibly make a profit, and it survived only because of Thaw's subsidy. If Brashear had understood how to estimate the average number of devices he had to make to produce one good one and the real cost of the labor, equipment, and legal risks involved in his enterprise, he would probably not have solicited orders for the very stringent specifications he regularly agreed to meet. Or he would have priced his devices beyond the means of the laboratories and observatories which most needed his work.

With any autobiography, the reader finishes with a set of questions which the author has not addressed fully. This is particularly true with Brashear's memoir, now nearly three-quarters of a century old, since our modern style favors frank discussion of disagreements, and Brashear was either a master diplomat or remarkably naive. One wonders about his wife, who worked side by side with him in their makeshift workshop for many years during an era when women were not encouraged to pursue such professional interests. One wonders too about the true personalities of the many famous people mentioned in these pages: Brashear treats almost every human being he ever met as kind, generous, and without blemish. Despite these questions and the absence of reflection on the meaning of his achievements for science and general culture, Brashear's breezy, enigmatic style is most engaging, and he provides the reader with a very agreeable and almost effortless tour of science, technology, and Pittsburgh at the turn of this century.

Brashear's autobiography first appeared in 1924, four years after his death. Its completion was presumably due to the efforts of W. Lucien Scaife, who is named as the editor on the original title page and whose editorial note appears at the end of the author's preface. The book was published by the American Society of Mechanical Engineers and is reprinted with their permission. This edition omits chapter 19, Brashear's account of his trip to the Orient in 1916, and chapter 20, a group of letters selected by the editor.

JAMES V. MAHER

PITTSBURGH, PA., 1987

FOREWORD

It is not fiction that thrills us most. The strangest thing in life is truth; the most romantic thing in life is man. So the nearer we approach the truth about a man, the closer we come to romance more strange and thrilling than fiction.

The story of "Uncle John" Brashear, as he was affectionately called by literally thousands, is above all a romance. So is the story of almost any successful man. America, the land where all men are presumably born free and equal, where the immigrant can attain to anything but the Presidency and the poorest native-born need stop not even at that, America is full of romances. But among them all stands a unique figure, the simple, kindly figure of John Alfred Brashear.

For here was a man who, in an age so commercial and materialistic that success is more often than not measured in dollars and cents, remained steadfastly true to an ideal of perfection with utter disregard of material gain or loss; a man who was blessed with a love of beauty which kept him continually striving the while it tempered him into a concrete expression of that love itself. His is a unique figure, not because he fought and won from life success in a chosen work, though he did that nobly, but because life gave her gifts to him so generously.

Talk with any one who knew him and you will hear, not what he did, but what he was. Remarkable, indeed, when you stop to consider that in the making of astronomical lenses and instruments of precision he was the peer of any man of his time, and this not in America alone, but in Europe as well. Crusty old scientists came to him first because his genius could aid them in their work; they returned because they loved him. The inexperienced amateur wrote to him hesitatingly for help, and a correspondence ripened into a deep friendship which produced important investigations and discoveries in the scientific world. He had the supreme gift of giving himself, and the world is immeasurably richer because he gave himself so generously. For great as was his genius, far greater was the man.

It is characteristic of Uncle John that in writing his autobiography he should minimize his own importance. This modesty was not assumed. It was a fundamental part of his character. As long as he lived he never felt that he deserved the honors life brought to him, nor could he understand why he was singled out to receive them. He accepted them with a childlike simplicity and, like a child, he was pleased. But he did not comprehend. So he wondered why for a little while, and kept on working.

It is indeed difficult to explain how this simple millwright of Pittsburgh became one of its most distinguished citizens and a figure of international importance. Granted that he was the foremost maker of astronomical lenses of his day; that he was a master in the art of making plane surfaces; granted that early in his career nearly every observatory in America and Europe, as well as some in the Orient, was using apparatus which he had made and that the boundaries of science were being continually widened through the perfection of his work; granted all this and more, yet it does not explain the unusual position which Dr. Brashear occupied the last quarter of a century of his life.

Mechanical genius he certainly had. His numerous technical papers undoubtedly contained valuable contributions to scientific knowledge. But genius of this kind cannot explain why a man without formal education should, in the twentieth century, be chosen Acting Chancellor of a large university, or why he should be selected by Andrew Carnegie to have such a large share in the work of making and executing the plans for the Carnegie Institute of Technology. Mechanical genius cannot explain why Henry C. Frick, when he wanted to give a half-million dollars for educational purposes in Pittsburgh, should have selected John Brashear to handle the fund, a man whose entire life had demonstrated his inability to grapple successfully with financial and business problems. There was a genius other than mechanical which made John Brashear Pennsylvania's "best-loved citizen," the intimate of millionaires and paupers, of scientists, educators, and untutored workmen, the friend of the newsboy, the natural, easy playmate of little blind children. It was the genius of a rare personality.

Who can describe the peculiar genius of personality? It is as mysterious and unfathomable as life itself — a deep well within us which reflects back to the world not only ourselves, but the imprint of every one whose life touches ours. Uncle John, with his gift of making friends almost instantaneously, naturally called forth the best in all he met, and his radiant personality reflected, above everything else, love. His chief charm lay not in the fact that he was different from his fellows, but in the fact that he was so very much like them. His sympathy and understanding were spontaneous expressions of his love for all humanity, his confidence that a wise Creator would not allow any of the creatures of His handiwork to be entirely unworthy.

Uncle John's career, in spite of limited schooling, is an inspiring example of the capacity of the human mind to gain knowledge from every available source, and of the human heart to radiate its light to every living creature within its range. He combined the ability to work consistently with a real love for the object of his labor, and an unquenchable desire to share it with every one who could be interested in it. His desire for a telescope was as much a yearning to acquaint the whole world with the beauty of the heavens as it was to see it himself. Much as he loved and revered his science of astronomy — and surely no man has ever loved it more — he said and he believed that "the science most worth while in this world is that of extracting sunlight from behind the clouds and scattering it over the shadowed pathways of our fellow travelers." He loved the stars; their beauty and sublimity fascinated him. But because he believed that "there is nothing that contributes more to the elevating and ennobling of the human and spiritual in man than the sight of some of God's beautiful work," he loved them infinitely better. When, late in life, he undertook to raise funds to build the new Allegheny Observatory he did not rest content until it contained a room where any individual, regardless of race, creed, or color, should be permitted to see and learn of his beloved starry heavens.

In an age like the present, when clever publicity so often envelops the less great in a protective aura of unapproachableness, it is sometimes forgotten that the truly great are supremely simple, and that familiarity with them breeds not contempt, but increased respect. The man who is great to those who know him best is great indeed, and John Brashear was great indeed! It is said that at one time six thousand students in Pittsburgh knew him familiarly as "Uncle John," many of them well enough to call upon him for help and advice. He bore the test of intimacy and close association with old and young alike. Nothing about him was unreal or assumed. The sincerity which made him a great man made him an equally great friend.

It is to the eternal credit of America that, in the year 1920, at the very time when lecturers and writers (particularly those from England) were finding in American civilization a worship and respect for nothing except the commercial and material, a simple millwright in Pittsburgh should have been accorded such honors and homage as are bestowed on few; that a man whose ideals commercialism never lowered should have such public respect paid him as is seldom witnessed in any country. Virtue may be its own reward. After all, why not? Still it is good to see the last years of a worthy life crowned with the honors it so well deserves. It is well to feel that there remains everlastingly in the heart of a man a deep respect for the qualities that a rampant commercialism may attempt to deride.

If those who are interested in the education of American youth want to place before them the inspiration of a modern life of love, work, and service, they will do well to

acquaint them with the story of John A. Brashear. For
his life, as he has written it, is youth speaking to youth,
and unless we who are older have hoarded the spark that
keeps age forever young, we shall find ourselves outside the
ranks of those who can best appreciate his delightful ex-
cursions into the past. Uncle John was all but eighty when
they placed his ashes beside those of his wife in a crypt in
the Allegheny Observatory, but the soul that passed on to
take its place among the elect of the immortals was a
youthful soul that maturity and accomplishment had
failed to age.

For Uncle John spring never lost its thrill. The return
of life to earth never lost its power to flood his being with
new vigor and fill him with the exuberance of youth. In
such moods he was compelled to find some form of self-
expression outside of the ordinary. One of the last springs
he spent on this "round old earth" he was seen emerging
from his door with a bucket of aluminum paint in one
hand and a good-sized brush in the other. The sunny
morning was no brighter than the expectant smile on
Uncle John's face. Out on the lawn were two urns which
the Allegheny Park gardeners for years kept filled with
plants and flowers for him. With a youthful step he
crossed to the urns and soon they were resplendent with
fresh paint. Uncle John returned to the house. Standing at the top of the front steps, his desire for self-ex-
pression still unsatisfied, his glance fell on an urn similar
to his own on the lawn across the street. Without con-
sulting the estimable but rather dignified ladies who lived
there, he proceeded to decorate their urn as he had done
his own. Recrossing the street he caught sight of the

letter-box on the corner which Uncle Sam had decreed
should be painted green, and in a few minutes it, too, was
wearing a new spring dress of aluminum paint.

Then he turned toward home again with paint still in his
can and enthusiasm still in his heart. He paused and
looked around, open to suggestion as to further decoration.
Now his eye rested on the police reporting box decreed by
the city of Pittsburgh to wear a coat of red. The inspiration of spring and the availability of paint were too much
for him, and the police reporting box, too, stood at last
resplendent and glorified in the sunlight. Then, the paint
and Uncle John both being exhausted, he returned to his
home and his desk satisfied.

It is regrettable to have to report that the city did not
take kindly to his innovation. In due time about three
yards of printed rules, notices, and a questionnaire came
from the Post Office Department, and two men, one with
a bucket of green and the other with a bucket of red paint,
restored the neighborhood to its accustomed appearance.
But the rebuffs of an unromantic government, enmeshed
in red tape and red paint, were not sufficient to kill the
enthusiasm of this youth of all but eighty years. He smiled
as he filed the unanswered questionnaire away, and retained to its fullest his inner urge to beautify the world
about him.

The story of John Brashear is the story of a boy who
loved the stars and who early determined that so far as he
was able the whole world should have an opportunity to
know the inspiring beauty of the heavens. In due time he
fulfilled his early determination, and he did it so thoroughly
that he never had time to grow old. One day the sun rose

and ran its full course. As it set in undimmed splendor, its last rays crept gradually and silently up and over the figure of a man whose whole life had been a reflection of its power and beauty. Surrounded by his loved ones, Uncle John lay at peace, bathed in the rose light of the setting sun. Undimmed in splendor, he too passed beyond with the fading day.

EDNA A. YOST

AUTHOR'S PREFACE

MANY dear friends have urged me during the past five years to put in printed form some reminiscences of my long life; and I promised one dear fellow, with uplifted hand, that I would do so. Now The American Society of Mechanical Engineers comes along and tells me I must do it. I see no way to refuse when this splendid body of men, who have made me one of their honorary members — placing me among a coterie of master-workers whose shoe-latchets I am unworthy to unloose — insist on my writing something of my life history.

Who will read my reminiscences if they are written? Perhaps a few who have known me for, say, half a lifetime; perhaps another few who are interested in my hobbies and who may get some word of encouragement, some helpful suggestion in the domain of the science I have loved so well; perhaps some fellow workman from the old rolling mill, machine shop, or glass works, who knew me as a greasy millwright, or passable mechanic — some dear fellows still living, who, as younger men, used to go down with me at lunch-time on a cold winter day, in the ash-pit of a rolling-mill furnace, to listen to my stories of the stars, as I pictured them on a piece of sheet iron with a lump of chalk; perhaps some few of the more than one hundred thousand who have listened to my lectures during the past forty years; or a few of my old Sunday-School scholars, still living, whom I used — wickedly — to take after Sunday-School to the little cottage on the South Side hills to show them the beauties of the solar spectrum in my library, as the light from a slit in my window-blind passed through that first bisulphide of carbon prism, made by my own hands. Or it may have been to show them a great sunspot, projected on the ceiling through my first telescope, made by "Ma" and me after three years of night labor; for at that period of my life, I had to gain a livelihood in the mill in the daytime.

Perhaps some of the good people will read these reminiscences who have been fellow workers in the domain of our beautiful science of astronomy and astrophysics and who have helped me to "push forward the frontiers of human knowledge." I may possibly count, too, on those who have urged me to this difficult task. I know my dear friends and loved ones, who gave me kindly sympathy and helpfulness through many years of hard work, will read what they know comes from away down deep in my heart.

But, after all, my one big hope is that my humble effort in jotting down these items from life's memorandum book may help some struggling soul to master some of the problems of life, and of the beautiful in science, which will contribute new chapters of discovery to the now unknown and help to make this old oblate spheroid move smoother on its axis. For, aside from all knowledge, all science, I have long ago learned that "it is worth while to do even the smallest kindness, as we go along the way. Nothing is lost, no dewdrop perishes; but, sinking into the flower, makes it all the sweeter."

The happiest days of my life have been spent in endeavoring to lend a helping hand to the other fellow;

whether he was a prince or a pauper, a savant, or a poor chap seeking for some little knowledge of things good and beautiful, a teacher of men, or a lover of kiddies; and while my love of the beauties of the skies has not abated one jot or tittle from the time I had my first view in my old home town to the day I write this paragraph, my chief joy has been to hand these beautiful things over to the other fellow, that he, too, might share in them.

JOHN A. BRASHEAR

PITTSBURGH, PA., 1912

Editor's note. During the remaining eight years of his busy life, Dr. Brashear worked intermittently on his Autobiography. The greater part of it was written on the veranda of the cottage at Muskoka Lake. It was unfinished at the time of his death, but he fortunately left such a wealth of personal correspondence that it has been easily possible to supplement truthfully the modest self-revelation, that "comes from away down deep in his heart."

We regret that we cannot thank, individually, the many relatives and friends of Brashear who have so generously contributed material to the work. Especial thanks are due to Martha C. Hoyt, whose close association with Dr. Brashear, as his secretary, during the latter years of his life, has enabled her to render invaluable aid throughout the progress of the work, and to Edna A. Yost, who wrote the Foreword.

The preparation of the book has been in charge of the following committee: Joseph Buffington, George Ellery Hale, Charles M. Schwab, Ambrose Swasey, Benjamin Thaw, and William Lucien Scaife.

A MAN WHO LOVED THE STARS

CHAPTER I

ANCESTRY AND BOYHOOD

I CAME into this "old round world" on the twenty-fourth day of November, 1840.

My birthplace was the old town of Brownsville, Pennsylvania, on the Monongahela River, about sixty miles south of Pittsburgh. From a critical investigation of my forebears made by my cousin, Mrs. Imogen Brashear Oakley, we know that the Brashear family emigrated from France in 1658, coming over with the Huguenots, and landing in Virginia. That same year they emigrated to Maryland, settling in Calvert County.

The records show that the original name of the family was Brasseuir. About 1700 it was changed by some of the descendants to Brashier; and about 1713 the name is recorded as Brashears.

My great-grandfather, Otho Brashear, emigrated from Maryland in 1775, coming to the present site of Brownsville with Thomas and Basil Brown. Thomas Brown purchased the land on which the town was laid out; and my great-grandfather married his sister. The town of Brownsville was not incorporated until 1815; in which year I find recorded the name of my grandfather, Basil

Brashear, as a member of the first Council. I also find that Basil Brown and Basil Brashear were elected to membership in the first vestry of the Episcopal Church of Brownsville, at a meeting held August 26, 1813; and I presume this Basil Brashear was my grandfather and Basil Brown his cousin.

I can remember fully sixty years ago visiting quite frequently the old burying-ground on the Commons, where were buried many of the early settlers of Brownsville. I never could find the grave of my great-grandfather; but that of Thomas Brown, who died March 18, 1797, always held a fascination for me.

By the side of Thomas Brown's gravestone are those of John H. and Archibald Washington, cousins of George Washington (in my early years said to be brothers), both of whom died of smallpox which broke out among a lot of slaves they were taking to Kentucky. The death of both these men occurred April 10, 1818. I write of this because I can well remember how interesting it was to us boys who went to school in the old red-brick schoolhouse, built on the Commons so dear to us as a playground, which adjoined the little cemetery. I must add, with considerable shame for the place of my birth, that when I visited the graveyard (we never called it a cemetery) in later years, I found some of the old tombstones used as a pavement in front of a stable.

My grandfather, Basil Brashear, owned a tavern or inn in Brownsville, on what is now called Market Street. Here he entertained Lafayette in 1825. Although my mother was only six years old at the time of his visit, she remembered — or it may be was told by older persons —

that she was one of the children who strewed flowers on the sidewalk where Lafayette walked to the tavern.

A story of the old tavern told me by my father may be worth recording. A company of soldiers on their way to the Mexican War stopped over in Brownsville. The officers were put up in the hostelry; the soldiers, or most of them, found accommodations in the barn; but some of their muskets, which had been left loaded, were stacked in the kitchen. During the night a storm passed over the town. A flash of lightning hit the kitchen, exploded the charge of powder in the muskets, and of course stirred up a general commotion in the hostelry.

The old stone tavern is still standing, and the room occupied by Lafayette was shown to me on the occasion of my visit to Brownsville on the one hundredth anniversary of the founding of the town.

I regret that I cannot trace the history of my family on my mother's side farther back than my grandfather and grandmother. Their birthplaces I am not even certain of, although, from the meager information I have been able to obtain, my grandfather, Nathaniel Smith, was probably born in Massachusetts, and my grandmother in Phœnixville, Pennsylvania.

It was my Grandfather Smith who first told me about the stars. Up until the time he moved to the South Side, Pittsburgh, in 1855, his humble cottage on Albany Road, just at the edge of the town of Brownsville, was a favorite haunt of mine. I can remember the well-thumbed volume of Dr. Dick's "Works" over which he spent so many happy hours. Indeed, it is no wonder that I imbibed a love of astronomy very early in life. Many were the stories told me by my grandfather of the great comet of 1843, one of the finest comets of the nineteenth century, and he and my mother often regaled me with accounts of the great meteoric display of 1833. I can well remember that he taught me the constellations when I was about eight years of age, and later presented me with his prized volumes of Dr. Dick's "Works" from which I obtained so much inspiration.

A love for the science of astronomy was but one side of my grandfather's character. He was an all-round mechanic, inventor, musician, student, and lecturer. Always of a religious nature, he frequently addressed religious gatherings. I am told that he spoke slowly, deliberately, and without emotion, impressing his audience with the fact that he was a profound thinker. Logic was the leading feature of his defense of the Christian religion and his love for astronomy shone through his discourses by his frequent references to the "starry heavens."

He loved music, too. He could play the piano, flageolet, flute, violin, and pipe organ, and he oftentimes would make his own musical instruments. He made an E-flat clarinet for me, which, alas, was burned in a fire that destroyed our home when I was a boy perhaps ten years of age.

Before moving to the South Side, Grandfather used to make trips on foot between Brownsville and Pittsburgh going from house to house mending clocks, watches, musical instruments, and machinery of all kinds, and tuning pianos. During these absences I frequently stayed with my grandmother and helped her with the chores and numerous small duties about the farm.

Although Grandfather made a good living, earning

oftentimes twenty-five dollars a week in the mill, he died a poor man, for he was generous to a fault. It is related that the daughter of one of the carpenters in the mill where he was employed was fond of music, but could not persuade her father to engage a teacher. Grandfather gave her lessons without pay — then lent her his own piano which the family took with them when they moved to another place.

My father, Basil Brown Brashear, known as "Brown" Brashear, was one of fourteen children of Basil Brown Brashear, and was born in Brownsville on November 21, 1817. He was a quiet man, and although he lived to celebrate his golden wedding in Pittsburgh, where he died December 30, 1890, he was not a strong or a well man. He had learned the trade of a saddler, a very useful business in his early days, as the old town of Brownsville was on the National Pike over which was transported all the freight from its eastern terminus to Wheeling, from whence it was carried by flat-boat or canal-boat to points on the Ohio River.

My mother, Julia Smith Brashear, was one of six children of Nathaniel Smith. When she was a girl she worked in the old cotton mills in Allegheny, in one of which Andrew Carnegie and his father worked when they came from Scotland. Mother's people lived near the old aqueduct,[1] and one day she fell in. Grandma saw her fall, and she ran, jumped in, and caught Mother just as she was going down for the third time and saved her life. Before her marriage to my father, Julia Smith was a school

[1] This suspension aqueduct was said to be the first important engineering work designed by the first John A. Roebling. Not a vestige of it remains to-day.

teacher, and, due to his long ill health, she pursued this occupation at intervals after her marriage.

My parents, having little of this world's goods, made many sacrifices to give their children a fair, common-school education. I, being the first-born of the family, was always expected to help my mother with her house-work; and my sister Ella, the next younger, and I did our share of the household tasks as best we could. Indeed, when I look back on those early days, I am not ashamed to say that I could wash and iron such things as pillow slips, handkerchiefs — the old bandana kind, now almost a thing of the past — and I was going to write napkins, but there were no napkins in our family in those days, and, for aught I know, none to grace the tables of our wealthier neighbors.

While my mother made all our clothes, aided now and then by her sister, my Aunt Mary, I do not remember that we were ever dressed otherwise than neatly and comfortably.

There were seven children who came to grace the home of my father and mother, of whom, as already stated, I was the oldest. Then came my sister Ella, my brothers William, Charles, Frank, and George, and my sister Mary, the youngest of the family. Brother Charles passed away at the age of seventeen; Sister Mary, who married James Stephens, an engineer, passed away in California, leaving a family of four children, all of whom are living as I write (1918).

All my brothers followed some kind of mechanical pur-suit, except my brother George, who has been a trusted employee in the shipping department of the Jones & Laughlin Company for almost thirty-four years.

My father and mother were both lovers of music. With a number of good fellows of Brownsville, my father organized the Brownsville Brass Band, of which he became leader in its latter days. There was another fellow, who, in its latter days, also became a member of the band. His name was John A. Brashear; and he had the honor of "playing" the bass drum. On one occasion we were invited to play at the commencement exercises of Jefferson College, at Cannonsburg on the National Pike. We traveled there on the old band-wagon, so well known in the early days of brass bands.

How well I remember the great reception they gave us on that occasion! And here, as the Frenchman would put it, is the dénouement of that story: In 1865 Washington and Jefferson Colleges united, with their headquarters at Washington, Pennsylvania. This institution has made a splendid record during its long history, and has graduated some of our most brilliant men in law, science, literature, etc. In 1902 Washington and Jefferson conferred upon me the honorary degree of LL.D., which at first I declined to accept, as I did not feel that I deserved such an honor. However, friends of mine and of the college importuned me to accept, and I could not get away from the arguments of President Moffatt, my friend of many years; so I accepted, but with many misgivings as to my worthiness. As I stood on the platform to receive the honorary degree from the hands of the president, I related to those present how I had posed there as a youngster in the capacity of a bass-drum beater, nearly fifty years before.

My interest in astronomy, as has been said before, commenced very early in life. I can vividly recall one incident that happened in the year 1849, when I was nine years of age, that made such an impression upon my youthful mind that I never afterwards lost my interest in the stars.

Squire Wampler, of McKeesport, then a small town some forty miles from Brownsville, brought a little telescope of his own make to our town and offered a view of celestial objects at a nominal charge which I do not now recall. My grandfather learned of his coming, and I was taken to have a view of the moon and of the planet Saturn, that beautiful ringed planet being in good position for observing, although the rings were only about half open.

Young as I was, the scenery on the moon and the rings of Saturn impressed me deeply. Although I have since seen more than four phases of Saturn's ring-system through several of the finest telescopes in the world, the entrancing beauty of that first sight has never been forgotten. I think just here it would be interesting to give a brief history of that first telescope in which I was privileged to look.

Squire Wampler was a lover of astronomy. Since he did not have the means to purchase a telescope, he undertook to make one for himself. He secured a piece of French plate-glass, but he was unable to get a suitable piece of flint-glass to match it. Finally a search in the glasshouse débris of the Bakewell Glass Works, destroyed in Pittsburgh's great fire in 1845, brought into his possession several very good pieces of this material. From one of these pieces of flint-glass, combined with the crown, he constructed an excellent object glass, and then, being a watch- and clock-repairer, he made a very good mounting for the telescope. He later made several larger telescopes.

Through the kindness of my friend, Mr. E. A. Houston of Pittsburgh, I was recently made the fortunate possessor of a four-inch telescope made by this old-time amateur astronomer, who, in later years, paid a visit to my little workshop on the hill, and gave me words of encouragement that I have not forgotten. The four-inch lens, which I have among my relics, is very nicely corrected for what is known as spherical and chromatic aberration; but is literally full of striæ, illustrating the difficulty of obtaining good optical glass at that time as compared with the wonderful products of German and French optical glass workers of these later days.

Of my school teachers I call to mind Mr. Chalfant, my Aunt Lucy Rheasa, Joshua Gibbons, and George Wilkinson. To the last two I owe all my later training in the common schools of Brownsville. The schoolhouse was a small brick building on the Jeffreys Common, as I believe it is called to this day, occupying the ground where recently has been erected a model union school of which the town of Brownsville may be justly proud. I have often told my friends of later years that, were the old schoolhouse still standing, I believe I could pick out the spot on the outside wall that I leaned against after having smoked my first and last cigar! It was called a "Lady Finger," and was warranted not to make anybody ill. My effort was made at recess. I have never forgotten the nausea that followed that first and last smoke.

There were two rooms in the old school building; Joshua Gibbons occupied one, George Wilkinson the other. As there was a door between the two rooms, classes at times changed rooms and teachers for special studies. I was very fond of both these teachers, for they had their hearts in their work. I did not often come under the tutorship of Mr. Gibbons (there were no "Professors" in our schools in those days) but some of my comrades considered him one of the finest teachers they ever had. Among his pupils I may name the Reverend Hudson Wilkinson, and Alexander Martin, who later became Governor of Kansas.

To the memory of my dear teacher George Wilkinson I never can pay the debt of gratitude I owe for the deep and abiding interest he took in the boys under his care. It seems to me, as I look back over my school days, that Mr. Wilkinson cared nothing for the time and trouble he gave to the coterie of boys who loved to sit under his instruction. Of that little crowd of good fellows, I recall Tom and John Walsh, both of whom became master mechanics of the highest order, and Will Sheets, who married my sister Ella. He also became a master mechanic, and was one of the organizers of the mechanical firm of Best, Fox & Company. My desk companion in that old red-brick schoolhouse was Richard Knox, brother of our honored Attorney-General under President Roosevelt and Secretary of State under President Taft.

I cannot refrain from placing on record the last time I saw the face of my beloved teacher George Wilkinson. I had kept in touch with him from the time I left his school until the day of his passing away. Our relationship was of the most delightful character during all those years. He had left a letter to his brother and sister, to be opened after his passing away. In that letter he made the request that his old pupil, John Brashear, should make the address at the funeral services. I could not do otherwise than carry out his wishes; but never have I had a more difficult duty to perform; for as I looked in the face of my dear friend, and remembered his years of patient toil and labor with that coterie of boys in order to make men of them, my heart was too tender, and my words too difficult of expression to say what I would love to say of one of earth's noblemen.

Many of those friends of my early days have gone on, and boyhood memories are becoming dimmer with the passing years. As I think back now of the childish pranks and fancies of those happy days, I often smile at the boy who was Johnny Brashear. My naturally investigative mind showed itself quite early in life, and Mother used to tell stories of how I planted feathers I had found in the hope that some day I might own a real live chicken. I remember how I used to try to catch the thunder in a box which I hung outside our door during a storm, and I never failed to leave my play to hang up this box when a storm approached.

But possibly the happiest memory of those early times is the memory of the days and nights spent under my beloved stars, when Grandfather Smith would gather us around him on the grass after supper, and fascinate us with his stories of the constellations. When it was dark, Grandmother would put an end to it by calling all us children in, and on many such a night, long after the other children had gone home or to bed, her watchful eye would detect my absence. "Where's Johnny?" she would say, and then would come to find me flat on my back on the grass where Grandfather had left me, watching the starry heavens, lost in speculation about those far-distant worlds, and dreaming dreams of the day when I should make a telescope better than Squire Wampler's to see the beauties and wonders of this old universe.

CHAPTER II

SEEKING A VOCATION: RELIGION AND MARRIAGE

In 1855, at the age of fifteen, I left the old brick school-house, and later that year went to Pittsburgh. My Grand-father Smith was employed at the time in the spike-manu-facturing department of Lewis, Oliver & Phillips. As he desired to give me a mercantile education, I became a pupil at Duff's Mercantile College, but with little ambition to study bookkeeping and its correlated branches. When-ever I had a spare hour, I assisted my grandfather by packing spikes for him.

After three or four months of study, I was graduated with a fair percentage to my credit and returned to Brownsville where I got a position in a grocery store. Soon tiring of this, I was offered a place to learn the printer's trade with the local newspaper, "The Browns-ville Clipper," then published by the well-known editor, Seth T. Hurd. But I could not stand for the epithet, "a printer's devil"; so I went, for a short time, with Mr. Price, the proprietor of an auction store, to learn too soon that a man with a fairly good reputation as a citizen did not scruple to sell goods that were defective or damaged; so I soon quit that job.

Now came the turning-point of my life, which, with the application of modern methods of vocational guidance, would doubtless have been reached much sooner and without the loss of valuable time and energy.

My father secured a position for me in which I was to learn a mechanical trade at the engine works of John Snowden & Sons in my native town. At the time of my apprenticeship to the pattern-making trade in these works, 1856, many steamboats were built in Brownsville and in the city of Pittsburgh.

It has always been a pleasure to look back on those days of my apprenticeship, for every one of the master mechanics — and there were master mechanics in those days — was kind to me, and I had every opportunity given me to do high-class work. There were but two apprentices in the pattern shop, my friend "Jackie" Niman and myself. I sometimes thought more favoritism was shown me than was shown Jackie; but we got on nicely together, and I say with pride that he became one of the finest mechanics of his day.

Often I was taken into the drawing room to assist in making drawings (there were no blueprints in those days), and not infrequently I was asked by Mr. Snowden's son Nelson to assist him in the office on pay-day. Later on in my apprenticeship, I was frequently called on to assist in putting the completed engines on the boats for which they were built. Both side- and stern-wheel boats were built in those days. I recall vividly the trying job it was to bore the holes for the bearings of the wheel-shaft in a side-wheeler — with back bent under the deck above, boring a hole ten to fifteen feet deep with an inch-and-a-half auger, in a space of, say, thirty inches; having to bore through solid timber at the top and oak braces underneath, and yet hit the string-pieces below, not over ten inches wide; pulling out the auger to clear it of chips every five minutes, through a hole bored in the deck above; and slipping the handle over the square shank every foot or eighteen inches. I can almost feel to this day the sore back that I carried home at night after a day at this task. I am certain that old-time river engineers will sympathize with the young apprentice who was put at this task.

My success in learning my trade and the use of tools was, in a large measure, due to the teachings of my Grandfather Smith, whose mechanical skill was of the highest order for his day. I had been his companion in his private workshop, where he constructed an electric engine, run by a Bunsen battery; made one of the finest Morse telegraph instruments constructed west of Philadelphia; and made, perhaps, the first gyroscopes in Western Pennsylvania. He had, complete and in operation, the first daguerreotype and other necessary apparatus for taking pictures, made in Brownsville or Pittsburgh.

I completed my apprenticeship in three years and accepted a position in Louisville, Kentucky, with the Dennis Long Company in 1859. There I helped to build the engines for the city waterworks that were erected in 1861. Here I was caught when the Civil War broke out, and Louisville was soon in such a state of unrest that business of nearly every kind was suspended. I found myself without a job, save that which served to keep me in food and clothing. I had sent all my savings to my parents, and was, in common parlance, a bankrupt; so when an undertaker came along and offered me a job making coffins, I accepted perforce.[1] Having mastered the use of

[1] In recalling experiences of these days, Dr. Brashear has told his friends that before he took the job with the undertaker, he made and

wood-working tools, I soon became quite expert at the job, gruesome as it seemed at first. However, it enabled me to earn money enough to return home; and I bade good-bye to my Southern friends, many of whom had been very kind to me during my stay in Louisville.

I reached Brownsville in July, 1861. After a visit to my home, where I found my father out of work, I immediately went to Pittsburgh where I secured a position as mechanic in the rolling mill of Zug & Painter. Soon afterward I was placed in charge of the machinery of the mill, where I remained until the great strike of 1867.

After I had completed my apprenticeship at Snowden's, my mother expressed a great desire that I should study for the ministry. I thought the matter over carefully and undertook to read and study books prescribed by the Conference of the Methodist Church, during the hours when I was not working. Watson's "Institutes," Butler's "Analogy," and Wesley's "Sermons" were in the curriculum. I studied them, or at least a part of them, with some interest; but I liked Whately's "Logic" better than any of the books mentioned, for it taught me the value of inductive reasoning, and this touched my love of the study of natural philosophy, as the sciences were then named. Upon examination, I was given a license as a local preacher;

sold blacking boxes. "Jackie" Niman had married and moved to Louisville a year before young Brashear went there. Mrs. Niman tells that she and "Jack and John" spent many happy summer evenings together in their yard in Louisville playing and singing, and that "John used to play the flute a great deal." These summer evenings in the Southland were almost the last leisure that he enjoyed before the hard days in the mill and the evenings devoted to study and the struggle for education which never ended until he passed away.

and for several years I devoted my spare time to mission work among my fellows, particularly while I was living in Louisville.

Many of my friends wished me to quit work as a mechanic and become a member of the Pittsburgh Conference of the Methodist Church. Others — some of my best friends, already in the ministry — told me this would be a great mistake, as my tastes were all in the direction of science, especially of astronomical studies and instruments. I remained undecided, all the time considering my mother's hopes that her eldest son should become a minister.

To me, the story of why I did not enter the ministry is one of the most painful incidents of my life. I had been asked to preach a sermon to the people of a certain church in Pittsburgh on a day when the minister was expected to be absent. I was working hard in the rolling mill at the time. Having chosen as my subject the first four verses of the first chapter of Genesis, I gave my talk on creation, as viewed from the scientific side; and, according to Dana's "Cosmogony of the Bible," quite in agreement with the story as recorded in my text. They listened to me with interested kindness, although I confess my knees trembled as I talked. Owing to unforeseen circumstances, my friend the minister did not go away and was, consequently, present with me in the pulpit. His remarks after I had finished were at first commendatory; but he closed with these cruel words that still ring in my ears: "But I do not think a knowledge of creation is necessary to the believer or the seeker for truth; for the Bible teaches us, if we believe, we shall be saved, and if we believe not, we shall be damned; and this is the sum and substance of the whole matter."

I cannot believe that his words were meant unkindly — no, I cannot believe they were — but, oh, how they hurt! I went home heartbroken. My dear wife offered all possible consolation, and afterward I heard kindly expressions of sympathy from members of the congregation who had heard my talk. But I never got over the "most unkindest cut of all"; and I never entered the ministry.

As I look back now on the narrowness of those early times, I rejoice that it has changed for a better and brighter view of a pure and undefiled religion. More than half a century has elapsed since that sermon on the beauties of creation, and in that time I have been asked to speak in the churches and chapels of almost every denomination — Jewish, Protestant, and Catholic — on topics of science that are so closely related to things good, beautiful, and ennobling. Regardless of race or creed, we may see in star and flower, in music and in art, in valley and mountain, aye, in ten thousand little things around us, the beautiful in God's creation. We have lived to see a brighter age, a better day. May I quote Ella Wheeler Wilcox's lovely words as I close this part of my story:

> So many Gods, so many creeds,
> So many ways that wind and wind,
> While just the art of being kind
> Is what the sad world needs.

I must not go further with this epoch of my life without recording the most cherished and the most important experience of all.

From early life I was an active worker in church, Sunday-School, choirs, and literary societies; and when I took charge of the machinery of the Zug & Painter mill in 1861, I became choir leader of the Sunday-School and church in the neighborhood. I had been there but a few Sabbaths when I became acquainted with a teacher by the name of Phœbe Stewart. In after years I learned from one of her pupils that her teacher said she was going to "set her cap" for me the very first Sunday I gave a little talk to the school.

Perhaps that was one of the most important episodes of my whole life; for an affection between us soon ripened into love, a love which abideth. A year of courtship, and we were married without ostentation on September 24, 1862.[1] We commenced our life together in the most humble manner, and the joy which cometh only from love kept us as sweethearts ever.

I had always given my earnings to my father and

[1] It may be worth while to explain the cause of young Brashear's marriage "without ostentation," as he termed it in the sunset of life. Thomas Stewart, the father of Phœbe, was much opposed to his daughter's receiving attention from Brashear, as he did not wish her to marry, although he did not object to the young man who was a boarder in his house.

Accordingly, on the evening of September 24, 1862, with the connivance of her brother Morgan and his wife, Phœbe and John went to the home of another brother, William Stewart, living near by and recently married, and, with her sister-in-law's wedding dress on, Phœbe was wedded to the man of her choice.

Planning to keep the marriage a secret, as they feared the displeasure of Mr. Stewart, they returned home without having been missed. The following day, while Phœbe was making pies for dinner, apple pies without a top being a special weakness of the groom, the latter entered the kitchen to bestow a kiss upon his bride. It was an unfortunate moment for them, for Mrs. Stewart entered at the same instant, and an explanation became necessary. It was followed by Mr. Stewart's anger, and the sudden beginning of housekeeping in Allegheny.

mother, so when we were married I had but little with
which to go to housekeeping. But the memories of those
early housekeeping days in three rooms are very sweet
to me now; and in later years we often recalled with
pleasure the many friends who were welcomed in that
little house. Most of them, alas, have gone over to the
Summer Land; and, as I write these lines my heartstrings
almost snap asunder with grief when I record that the
sweet spirit, who was my guiding star through half a
century of as happy a married life as was ever vouchsafed
to man, was taken from me some years ago, her dear life
going out, after years of suffering, like the sinking of a
summer sun. The record of that pure, unselfish, loving,
patient life can never be told in words, but it is written
upon my heart, never to be effaced.

When we were married, as already stated, we started
life in a very humble way, first renting three rooms in
lower Allegheny. But getting across the Ohio River to my
work in winter proved difficult and even hazardous; for the
river was often full of running ice, and occasionally was
frozen over. So we gave up our first home in the spring
(1863) to move to an old house close to the mill of Zug &
Painter where I was employed. We put the house into
livable shape. The yard was all cinders from an old smelt-
ing furnace; but I put a fence around it, and wheeled nearly
a hundred loads of dirt from under an old stable in the
neighborhood. Here Ma and I raised our lettuce, radishes,
and onions, and were happy. Grandfather Smith spent
every Sunday with us, as he was working at that time in
Birmingham for Lewis, Oliver & Phillips, and we frequently
talked over astronomical matters during these visits.

As he was then well on in years, my wife always spent an hour "making Grandpa look nice," as she expressed it. How he did enjoy having her comb his hair, trimming it if need be! And how we missed him when he returned to his home in Brownsville! A year or two later I was called there to help lay him away in his last resting-place. I have mentioned before the pleasant and helpful relationship between my grandfather and myself, and my one regret is that he did not live to see the heavens in a telescope made by the boy to whom he had given his inspiration and love for the good and beautiful.

CHAPTER III

ASTRONOMY AND MUSIC

DURING my six years' stay with Zug & Painter (1861–67), I made studies of the constellations, particularly on Saturday nights, after the fires and smoke of the mills had ceased to darken the sky. I would then take my Barritt's Star Map, get between the piles of pig metal out on the river-bank, and, with a candlelight, locate positions on the map.

Unfortunately, the hill on the south side of the river prevented me from seeing the more southern constellations; so frequently, when the water was low enough, I rowed across in a skiff to a bar on the other side of the Ohio, and there I could see much more of the heavens than was possible on the South Side, among the piles of pig metal.

Later on I purchased a lot on top of the hill which Ma and I tried to cultivate, but made a failure of, not for want of hard work, but evidently because we were not intended to be farmers. However, it was a fine place to view the heavens and, although it was a stiff climb to get there after a hard day's work, it always gave me "full value received."

An incident occurred one night while I was out on the river-bank studying the stars, which is perhaps worth relating. The Pan-Handle Railroad had been finished only a year or two, as I remember, and it ran along a cut in the hillside, from what was then called Temperanceville to South Pittsburgh. Owing to the fact that there were frequent landslides all along the hillside, especially when the frost was coming out of the ground in the springtime, the watchmen were supposed to be constantly walking along that part of the track. About eleven-thirty one night in March, I heard a fearful crash above the mill, rocks evidently falling upon the roof. I suspected at once what had happened; and, leaving my iron-bound observatory, I went up the hill as fast as my legs would carry me. I found at least a hundred feet of the track covered with fallen earth and rocks from the hill above. I at once rushed to the station at the west end of the track, where I found the watchman asleep with his lighted lantern beside him. He was not long in sending an alarm; and while no train passed the landslide that night, I have often wondered if my night orgies, studying the stars, prevented a railroad accident, which, alas, happened all too frequently in those days.

The great strike of the iron-workers — that is, the "puddlers" — was instituted early in 1867. I was instructed by my employers to put the machinery of the mill in good order, and then await the settlement of the strike. Although I was supposed to be working by the year, my wages were stopped; and since I had put all my savings into the purchase of the lot on the hill, I was in rather a bad fix financially.

In the midst of my perplexity as to how I should make ends meet, I learned of a position as millwright with McKnight, Duncan & Company in Birmingham, now

South Side, Pittsburgh. A visit to Mr. McKnight settled
the matter at once; and, although reluctant to leave my
old employers, I accepted the offer and at once moved to
Thirteenth Street, Birmingham, where we soon found congenial friends and neighbors.

Many interesting events of church and social life were
enjoyed in the next few years. Wherever we went we continued to seek musical friends, and I had the honor of
being selected as the choir-leader of the old Bingham
Street Methodist Church. I found time to study Tindel's
"Thorough Bass," "Thorough Bass without a Master,"
and Wolfhart's "Composition of Melodies"; but I ventured upon only a few compositions, which I tried upon
my wife, who had a lovely soprano voice. My own was a
mongrel sort of tenor, and had been practically ruined by
trying to lead all the parts when the singers got into
trouble.[1]

The effect of my compositions poorly performed upon
the reed organ was to put my wife to sleep, so I never
ventured to try them on the public. However, I got much
pleasure from teaching singing classes the rudiments of
music, which had been so thoroughly taught me and my
schoolboy friends by George Wilkinson.

At about this time I helped to organize a Cantata Society, made up of the different choirs of Birmingham.
Our organist and pianist was Lida McIntosh, an accomplished artist, and one who helped to make our society a
success, now and then assisted by William Ruhe, a master
on the 'cello. These two lovers of music became lovers of

[1] On the contrary, his voice was naturally sweet and melodious even at
an advanced age.

each other and married later on. We had some fine voices in the old Cantata Society, and Ma and I made friends who remained dear to us throughout life.

It would require no great stretch of memory to fill several chapters with these few years of happy married life; for, outside our home duties, our church work, our interest in benefit concerts, and my own hard work in the rolling mill, it was also the epoch when we decided to buy a lot and build ourselves a home.

Please let it be understood that I did not shirk or neglect my work in the rolling mill during the nearly seven years that I was with McKnight, Duncan & Company, for I am proud to say that not only were my employers satisfied with my devotion to their interests, but like my former employers, Mr. Zug and Mr. Painter, they took me into their confidence in many matters, and I was a welcome visitor at their homes.

During my stay with McKnight, Duncan & Company, the mill was burned to the ground by the carelessness of a workman who upset his lamp in a barrel of oil. The fire started at five A.M., and not only was the building destroyed, but much of the machinery was totally ruined.

I had heard the alarm, and was on the spot as soon as my legs would carry me there; but I could do nothing toward saving the building or machinery. I was grieved beyond measure, and dreaded to meet the senior member of the firm. What a relief it was to me when he finally came and told me not to worry, as the mill was old, some of the machinery antiquated, and that they had been thinking of rebuilding at some future time, anyway! Moreover, they had a fair insurance, and the only real matter of concern was the delay in filling their orders. I shall never forget his words as we parted that morning: "John, you have a big job before you to rebuild the mill, do away with the old machinery, etc.; so I want you to watch and pray over your task." "But," he added, "don't take both jobs; you do the watching, I'll do the praying."

The fire occurred in the late fall,[1] so I had a winter's work before me. Fortunately, it was a mild winter, and we made splendid progress, eliminating the gear-driven small mill, using the modern method of driving by belts, eliminating the square shafting on which were keyed fly-wheels and heavy gear-wheels, with wood packing, iron wedges, etc.

On the first of the following May we were ready to start anew. The carpenters had finished the building, and all was ready. It was an exciting moment. Everything went off beyond my most sanguine expectations, with not a hitch in the new engines, boilers, mills, shears, etc. The firm, headed by Mr. McKnight, came out of the improvised office to see the start of the rejuvenated mill, and they were delighted.

A little later on Mr. McKnight came into the mill again, and after telling me how pleased he and his partners were at the result of the rehabilitation of the works, he said they had decided to raise my wages three hundred dollars a year, and date the raise back to January 1st. Then, handing me a check for one hundred dollars, he told me to go off and take a week or ten days' vacation with my wife.

What an adventure this seemed to us! Neither Ma nor I had ever been more than sixty miles from our birth-

[1] December 8, 1871.

places and we had never seen a large body of water. We decided to go to Cleveland and Put-in-Bay, where we should have a chance to see Lake Erie.

On the way we purchased a Cleveland paper, and in the advertisements we located a boarding-house near the lake shore. We were put into a miserable room next to the street, and got very little rest the first night on account of the heat. There was no ventilation, but plenty of mosquitoes. The following morning we found more pleasant quarters. We enjoyed trips around the city in horse-drawn cars, and about the middle of the week we took our trip to Put-in-Bay, leaving our little daughter Effie with the landlady. The lake was comparatively quiet and I do not remember that we became seasick. We surely enjoyed it, as we both loved the water.

Soon after returning from our trip, we began to prepare for the building of our new home. We had purchased on May 28, 1870, two lots, each twenty-five by one hundred and fifty feet, on the hillside above Twenty-Second Street, South Side. Part of the lots was pretty steep, but there was a fine view over the hills, Monongahela River, and the busy mills, and Ma and I had designed a plain but pretty house to be built there. We found we must give up our interest in concerts, etc., much to our regret; but we knew it would require every spare minute of our time if we were to give the necessary attention to the building of our cottage. So, saying good-bye for a time at least to our musical interests, we ordered the lumber. It was hard to get it up the hill in those days, with such miserable roads and steep climbing, but we got on wonderfully well, for some of the mill boys gave us a hand with the heavy work.

There was an immense oak tree on one of the lots which we used for the posts on which the house was built. I cannot remember at this late day how these heavy posts were handled, those deep holes dug, and the foundation sills placed on them; but I was there every evening until the darkness came on, as our hope was to get into the home before cold weather set in. The mill boys helped me to put up the frame after I had all the studding ready. A carpenter helped me put up the siding, but my wife and I did a goodly share of this work, and also the laying of the floors.[1]

It was a happy day when we moved into our new home. Although it was little more than a shell, it was *home;* and I well remember Ma's suggestion that we have a supper for the mill boys who had helped us through the summer and early autumn. We had not yet dug our cistern, so the boys came up early, and in a jiffy they had the pit dug deep enough to receive its cement. Then the supper was served; yes, we called it supper in those days, and as Ma was a master cook, she had some bully good things to eat. I remember there was oyster soup to start with, and that one of the boys, who had never tasted the "luscious bivalve" before, had to leave the table hurriedly. He came back, however, and finished the other good things provided by the master caterer.

The fall and winter evenings that year were devoted to making the inside of our new home as comfortable as our

[1] The photograph on the opposite page shows this home at No. 3 Holt Street, Pittsburgh, as it now appears. It is owned by the Brashear Memorial Association and, as "The House of Inspiration," serves as a social settlement and Brashear Museum. A plate on the door quotes Brashear thus: "Somewhere beneath the stars is work which you alone were meant to do. Never rest until you have found it."

ability and our resources could afford. My father, who was working as gate-keeper in the new mill, stayed with us through the winter, and helped us with many little pieces of work, such as tacking on the paper plastering which we used as a temporary lining in three of our rooms to keep us from freezing during the winter months. This served us very well until a storm came up one night the following spring, and the wind, getting under the unprotected basement, ripped all our patent plaster off and left us in quite a dilemma. It also blew our house four or five inches out of plumb. But we were able to straighten it up, and lived in it quite comfortably this way for another year, when we finished the lower part — that is, four rooms and the hallway.

It was a hard task to get to and from our work that first winter; indeed, for several winters. Snow and ice would form on the hillside, and then we often had to slide down over the steep places, to get to the road and steps that led us down to the borough roads. Before moving to the hill, I had helped my old friend Mr. Goff to organize a Sunday-School in a schoolhouse at the upper end of Birmingham, which later developed into the Walton Methodist Episcopal Church. My wife and I were both interested in this work, and we were always ready for our Sunday trips down the hill. How we ever got up and down on some of those wintry days, with snow and ice on the hillside and danger at every step, I do not know. But I am perhaps forgetting that I had reached only my thirtieth year when we moved to our new house, and my wife was several years younger.

It can easily be seen that my time outside of my long

working hours at the mills was pretty well occupied during
the early years of my married life. But I still found precious hours in which to read. As soon as I had my own
rooftree over my head, I began to lay the foundation for
my growth in scientific knowledge — my library. It con-
sisted of a few books on a couple of shelves suspended by
wire in my bedroom, and I used to read far into the night.
Clothes were luxuries I could economize on. I rarely ever
bought a whole suit at one time. But books had become
necessities. I can still hear Ma, our family treasurer,
when I came in with a book which we could ill afford to
buy, saying gently, "All right, Lunny; but remember we
can't afford to buy another one this week."

CHAPTER IV

MAKING THE FIRST TELESCOPE

WHEN we moved into our new home, one of our first thoughts was to build a little shop and commence the construction of a telescope. I had never lost the interest in astronomy which Grandfather Smith had aroused in my early boyhood, and I had determined that at some time I would have a telescope of my own. I thought, also, how nice it would be if there were a telescope or a place where the layman, boy or girl, could have a chance to look at the stars, the moon and the planets, little dreaming that in my later life I should have an opportunity to help bring this very miracle to pass.

In earlier years I had gone to see an optician, so-called, in Pittsburgh by the name of Shaw, to find out what the cost of a good telescope object glass would be. He discouraged me by saying that, if I bought the lens from him, I should not know how to mount it or how to use it. The result was that I ordered a glass for a five-inch lens from Heroy & Marrenner, New York agents for Chance Brothers, of Birmingham, England. In the mean time, a friend by the name of Peter Reid loaned me a two-inch telescope, mounted on a little tripod. I used this every night I had an opportunity, while I was waiting for my glass. One evening, while I was observing, my favorite cat "Bolivar," who was educated to do quite a number of tricks, ran up over the chair on which I was sitting, over

my shoulder, and out to the end of the telescope, up-
setting it and badly injuring the tube, but fortunately not
breaking the glass.

As I had no facilities at the time for repairing the tube,
I took it to an optician in Pittsburgh by the name of
Stieren, who repaired it nicely so that I was enabled to
return it in very good condition to Mr. Reid. I mention
this because that little incident was the beginning of a
friendship with Mr. Stieren, who was a real optician, that
remained throughout his life. I have often found that
little instances of this kind, if appreciated, make for
friendships that are worth while in this world.

I had determined to make a telescope, and had ordered
the glass for it. The next step was to find a suitable place
to work in. Instead of building a workshop, I bought from
my next-door neighbor a little house, eight and one-half
by ten feet, which he had built for a coal house. I designed an engine and purchased a small boiler for it.
These I placed in a little shed adjoining the workshop.
Then I constructed a bench for a small second-hand lathe
I had bought, and we had a pretty fair amateur outfit.

Our glass arrived from New York, and my good wife
and I went to work at it with all the zeal and interest of
children with a new toy. This was in 1872. Our work
was, of course, done in the evenings. At that time I
usually got up at about five-thirty in order to get to the
mill on time. I would not get home until about six o'clock,
often much later if there had been any kind of a breakdown in the mill. When I arrived, I would always find
steam raised, the shop immaculately clean, everything in
order, and a good supper on the table. After the dishes

were washed, Ma would always come out and help me; and we have often worked until twelve, one, and sometimes as late as two o'clock in the morning, although our better judgment would often prompt us to go to bed.

When we began work I was absolutely ignorant of the various processes used in lens-making, but I managed to cut the square disks to circular form, and roughly to compute the curves, although I knew nothing about a study of the index of refraction or dispersion of the glass. Many, many trials did we have in those years of grinding and polishing. Just as we would approach a time when we thought we could polish the surface, we would get a scratch on it, and it would have to be done over again. One evening when I had one of the surfaces in pretty good shape to be polished — and by the way, I made the grinding and polishing tools myself — I had the misfortune to drop the crown lens. It broke in two pieces, and broke my heart, as well as my wife's, in a good many hundred pieces!

An English friend of ours who happened to be there at the time of the accident asked for the privilege of replacing the disk. This he kindly did, but it required two months to get it from England. Then the work of getting it into circular form and grinding it to the curves all had to be done again, but it proved to be a very good piece of glass, as results showed afterwards.

Finally we had the five-inch lens ready for mounting. My brother-in-law, Will Sheets, who was a pattern-maker by trade, made the wooden part of the tube for me. We started to make the lens to be about six feet focus; and while the color correction was very nearly right, it had a very serious over-correction for spherical aberration. So the tube was made nine feet long. I made the patterns for the brass parts of it myself, had them cast, and turned them myself in the old lathe, to fit the glass and the draw-tube end.

I shall never forget the night that we mounted this tube temporarily in our room that looked to the south, stuck the telescope out of the open window, and pointed it to the planet Saturn, which was then in very good position for observing. For three years we had labored lovingly at our task, and now we were to enjoy the fruits of our labor. Although the spherical aberration was barely corrected, yet the view that I had of the planet that night is pictured vividly in my mind to-day, as is that first view that I had of the same planet in the little telescope belonging to Squire Wampler, through which I had my first view of the heavens in old Brownsville. After my wife and I had enjoyed the sight, we could not rest until we had called in some of the neighbors; and while it was anything but the perfect glass that later studies told us was absolutely necessary if we were to have the kind of instrument that would come up to the standard, nevertheless, we had some very interesting views of the moon and other objects that did not demand such perfection in the glass as the images of the stars.

Our next job was to construct a mounting for the telescope. This did not take very long, as I found an iron column at McIntosh & Hemphill's Works, near the mill. The equatorial parts were made by my own hands; and a large opening was cut in the roof of our cottage so that we could command a fairly good portion of the heavens. But we had to wait for the stars, planets, and moon to come to us, which we were willing to do.

I had now, in the spring of 1876, come to a place in my work and studies where I plucked up courage to write to Professor Samuel Pierpont Langley, who had charge of the Allegheny Observatory, asking permission to bring the object glass to the Observatory that he might inspect it and perhaps give me advice about further improving it. I received a gracious reply from him, suggesting a night on which I should call at the Observatory to see him. I immediately prepared for this visit, and I must confess I was greatly excited at the prospect of having one of my dreams come true. How many times as I lay out on the cinder banks by the river-side after the mills had stopped running, studying the stars when the smoke had cleared away, I had dreamed of the distant day when I might see the heavens through the telescope that I had heard had been erected in the Allegheny Observatory! Many and many a Saturday afternoon I had climbed to the top of "Coal Hill" just to look over at the dome of that observatory — to look and to dream. For not only did I desire the privilege of seeing the beauties of the heavens myself; I dreamed of a day when all mankind, every boy and girl, might have that privilege, too.

There were no cars running at that time out Perrysville Avenue to the Old Observatory, near the present Langley Avenue — indeed, there were none for many years afterward — and I had the misfortune to lose my way. But at last I arrived at the door of the Observatory, rang the bell, and was ushered into the presence of the man whose friendship I enjoyed from that night to the end of his life.

As he took the lens in his hands and scrutinized its polish and general make-up, I stood trembling before him. At last (and to me, at least, it was a long time coming) he said, "Mr. 'Brazier,' you have done very well"; and then he asked me the character of the curves. When I had told him, he suggested that I should have had an easier task had I made them after the general plan used by the Clarks.[1] He asked me if I had any books on the subject of telescope construction; and on my replying in the negative, he went to his private collection of books and brought me a copy of Dr. Draper's work on "The Construction of a Silvered-Glass Telescope and Its Use in Celestial Photography." He told me to keep it as long as I wished; but as he valued it very highly, he asked me to be sure to return it to him.

I learned from him that evening that he and his brother John, a professor of chemistry, whose friendship I was happy in acquiring later on, had made a six-inch reflecting telescope in the barn at their father's home; and I could see that he appreciated the difficulties we had encountered in making the five-inch object glass.

Fortunately for me, it was a clear night, and Professor Langley asked me if I would like to have a look in the thirteen-inch telescope of the Observatory. At last I was to have the fulfillment of the wish I had so long cherished!

The planet Saturn was still in good position for observing. The thirteen-inch refracting telescope was placed upon the beautiful planet, the clock-work started, and I had my third view of the queen of all the objects in the

---

[1] Alvan Clark and his sons, possibly the foremost makers of optical surfaces of that day.

heavens. Wonderful! Could I ever make a telescope that would show its ring-system, its belts, its satellites, like that?

At first I felt a sort of discouragement when I contrasted my view in this masterpiece with that in our own telescope, but the feeling did not last long, and as I bade my new-found friend good night, I went away with a grateful heart, and with a new incentive and a higher ideal before me.

How I devoured the pages of the book he loaned me! Yes, I think it was read through before I slept any that night, as it was Saturday night and I could sleep longer on Sunday mornings.

Before I finished reading the book, I had decided not to go any further in the correction of the five-inch lens. Until my talk with Professor Langley that night I had not known how much simpler it was to make a reflecting telescope, as that did not require high-grade and costly optical glass, and had but one surface to be corrected, though that one must be even more accurate than the surfaces or curves of the object glass. So I decided to keep the five-inch lens, as it was, for my observing until we could make the larger-sized reflecting telescope.

That first visit to the old Allegheny Observatory had a profound effect upon all my life. It was my introduction to the larger world of science and the beginning of my friendship with men who found their greatest happiness in discovering nature's hidden truths in spite of poverty, isolation, and increasing work of body and mind. In my half-century's work and interest in scientific matters, I have known scores of scientists personally, and other

scores through long correspondence, and all, all have
helped me in one way or another to master some of my
problems. It has been a rare occasion, indeed, when I have
met rebuff in my constant seeking for knowledge and
asking for help. There is no room for the mean man, for
a small soul, in the scientific world, and the memories of
my friends in this profession are to-day treasures of greater
worth than gold or precious stones.

CHAPTER V

LIFE IN THE IRON MILLS

DURING most of the twenty years (1861–81) that I spent in the iron mills of Pittsburgh I was employed as a millwright, in those days one of the hardest and most trying of all the positions in a rolling mill. My employment with McKnight, Duncan & Company terminated while I was at work on my first telescope, for the business panic of 1873 forced them to close their works. I was fortunate, however, in finding a position in the mould shops of Adams & Company, glassware manufacturers, only a few blocks farther away than the mill. Mr. Adams was a friend of mine and a splendid man; and, like all the men in the mould shop, was very kind. While the work was not familiar to me, my previous knowledge of the use of tools soon enabled me to do fairly good work in turning "plungers," etc.; and the knowledge gained in that shop was invaluable in my little workshop on the hill, when turning the tools for grinding the lenses for the new telescope. The boys of that mould shop I can never forget for their kindness in instructing me in the use of the lathe, and in close and accurate fitting of the moulds.

I had been with Adams & Company but a few months when Charles Zug, of the firm of Zug & Company which had severed its connection with the old firm of Zug & Painter, my original rolling-mill employers, came to ask me to accept the position of millwright in their mill over in the city.

At first I hesitated, for although the increased wages were an inducement, it meant a greater distance to go to work, which also meant getting up earlier in the morning, and of course going to bed earlier, and this meant taking some of the time that I wanted to devote to my telescope. However, at my wife's advice, I accepted the position, leaving Adams & Company and my associates there with great reluctance.

I have mentioned the fact that a millwright in my day had one of the hardest and most trying positions to fill in a rolling mill. I have gone into the mill on a Thursday morning and worked, with very few intervals of rest, until twelve o'clock Saturday night. When a breakdown in the machinery took place, it had to be repaired in the quickest possible time, as men were thrown out of employment, iron-melts wasted, and orders remained unfilled.

Moreover, in my earlier days there was much of the old type machinery, gear-wheels and fly-wheels fitted to square shafting, with iron wedges to center them on the shafting. Many, many nights I worked all night fitting a gear tooth in place of one broken during the day, the blacksmith having made one of wrought iron to a pattern always kept on hand. My mechanical friends will understand that the new tooth had to be beveled lengthwise, and, at the base, a snug driving fit made of it. Of course, the tooth had to be carefully filed to shape after it had left the hands of the blacksmith, and, when in place, had to have the accurate pitch. It was a nice job to fit a tooth in a straight gear, but a nicer one to fit it in a bevel or mitre gear. Most of the gear-wheels so fitted were of heavy pitch, four and one-half to six inches, and ten to twelve inches face.

It was my ability to do such work as this well and rapidly that earned my first position as millwright. Very shortly after I was married, while working as a mechanic for Zug & Painter, their manager asked me if I could put a tooth in a large spur-wheel.

"Yes," I replied, "if you will give me two good men who can handle a sledge, I will have the mill running in three hours."

"If you can have it running in twenty-four hours we will consider it a fine job," he answered.

I made the pattern, took it to the blacksmith, gave him full instructions as to material, etc., and had the mill running in three hours.

When the engine was started, the manager came to me and said, "Johnny, you are our millwright from this on," and he generously increased my wages from ten dollars to twenty-five dollars a week.

However, the real climax would come when a break occurred under the "squeezers," particularly the type used in Zug's mill; as the big machine, weighing many tons, would be almost red-hot overhead. I worked under them many times with a couple of assistants until we were completely exhausted and soaked with perspiration.

Even these memories, though, are not unmingled with pleasure. I remember one occasion when I was still with Zug & Painter when the mill's "squeezer" broke down, requiring repairs ordinarily taking at least three days. I worked day and night, and the mill was running again

in two days. Mr. Painter was so pleased that he came to
see me personally, offering me a present and the permission
to choose what it should be. I chose a silk dress for Ma!
It was green silk and cost him fifty dollars.

When I went with Zug & Company in 1873, I found
that Mr. Zug had greatly improved his mill from the days
of our early experiences. There was no square shafting,
no fly-wheels with wooden arms, no wooden timbers under
the engines and roll-housing foundations; and yet I can
remember when it was considered almost a sacrilege to
put anything under a mill or engine except great oak
timbers that were brought, a year or more before the time
needed, from the upper Monongahela River at the time of
its spring rise.

All this has gone into past history. Eight to ten years
was the life of a wooden foundation, which meant renewal
that often. It is now a thing of the past; but the remem-
brance of those hard, hot days and nights of repair work
can never be forgotten. I remember we used to stop two
weeks for general repairs in August. I think, hot as it
might be outside, it was a paradise when compared with
the inside of the mill during the time it was running.

I must not forget to record a terrible disaster which
occurred during my stay with Zug & Company. In the
late spring of 1876, the year of the Centennial Exposition
in Philadelphia, everything was running so smoothly at
the mill that I had asked the privilege of visiting the Exposition. There were some large telescopes being exhib-
ited there which I wished to see. My wife had expressed
a desire to visit the mill to see them making nails before
we went to Philadelphia, however, so I arranged for her

to come over one morning and bring Harry, our little boy, with her. Those were the days of the slow horse-cars. It was time for them to appear.

While awaiting their arrival, I was passing through the mill. The roller at the "muck" mill called my attention to a "fore plate" which he wished me to change slightly for him. I went at once to the room where I kept the patterns, carried the proper one to the roller, got his directions for the change he wished to make, and walked about forty steps to the little shop where I could alter the pattern. Just as I was fastening it in the vise, a terrific explosion occurred. I rushed out of the shop, but could see little for the dust, except that the roof of the mill had been torn off. I could see no one. I can explain this only by the fact that I must have been stunned for a short period.

I was soon brought to my senses, however, and rushing into the old office just across from the workroom, I looked for the fire-alarm key, but could not find it. Then I rushed outside the mill, and the first dreadful sight that met my eye was the mutilated body of a workman lying in the street. Alas, I soon learned that the boilers in the nail mill had blown up and had killed and wounded a number of my fellow workmen. Many were made cripples for life.

But what of my wife and boy? I was stupefied, horrified by the dreadful scene, and the uncertainty of the safety of my loved ones increased my agony. I had been in many sad accidents in the rolling mill, and had seen single lives crushed out, but this awful calamity unnerved me completely and totally unfitted me to be of any help to the unfortunate victims. It was something that had never happened to me before. It affected me all the more when I learned that the poor fellow who, half a minute before the explosion had asked me to fix the plate for him, was killed by the falling of the big crane on the very spot where we had been standing.

I learned afterward that my wife and boy were on their way to the mill and were crossing the bridge at Tenth Street when the explosion occurred. Had they taken an earlier car, they might have been with me in the nail mill and among the victims of the explosion.

As it would require considerable time to settle matters of insurance and get ready to reconstruct the mill, my employers insisted that I take the trip to Philadelphia to see the Exposition, as I had never had such a privilege in my lifetime, and this would perhaps help to get my thoughts away from the dreadful experience that I had passed through. I saw many things at the Exposition of great interest to me, especially the big telescopes, instruments of precision, the big Corliss engine, etc., but I could not dismiss the thoughts of my fellow workmen who had lost their lives in the explosion, and of others who were suffering from it, so I did not stay very long in Philadelphia.

My visit to the Exposition gave me, however, a new incentive to go on with my work on the proposed telescope; and as I look back now I think it was well that my hobby persisted at that time, as it in a measure took me away from the thought of the calamity at the mill.

The reconstruction of the mill was a difficult task for me, much more so than rebuilding the McKnight-Duncan mill on the South Side, as I so frequently had to tear down and rebuild a piece of machinery where some poor fellow had lost his life.

During all this period I am writing about we did not forget our church and other duties, although we were occasionally gently informed that we were giving too much time to things of a worldly character. Once in a while I got to the mill just a little later than my employer. Now and then, when everything was going well in the mill, I would slip off a little early, but I do not remember ever neglecting my duties or having complaints; in fact, I certainly had the friendship of all my fellow workmen, and more than one winter noon-hour I have spent with a lump of chalk and an old piece of sheet iron giving little talks on astronomy to the boys after they had emptied their dinner buckets. We used to make trips from the ash pit to the stars during those precious hours.

I also made a very interesting study, while in the mill, of the formation of little craters and other forms in the cooling slag from the puddling furnaces, where I had noted a wonderful similarity in miniature to the crater forms on the moon. Indeed, I was able at times, when conditions were favorable, to reproduce some remarkable formations in the cooling slag, almost identical in miniature with those I had studied on the moon's surface.

I had the temerity to write to a professor at the United States Naval Observatory about my study and experiments on furnace slag; but I never received an answer to my letter, as I have no doubt he sized me up for a crank. In later years that man gave me my first order for a spectroscope, and we became intimate in our friendship which lasted to the end of his life, but I never told him I was the fellow he did not write to.

Curious as it may seem, many years later William H. Pickering, who had heard of my studies in cooling slag, came purposely to Pittsburgh and made a journey with me to one of the few rolling mills that were making iron then by the old puddling process, and had the pleasure to witness the action of a cooling mass of slag, similar to the many I had studied.

Fortunately, I had saved one of the miniature slag craters, protecting it from breakage by placing it in a neat case and pouring plaster of Paris around the slag formation. At the request of Professor Pickering, the crater was cut through the center by the aid of a circular saw charged with diamond bortz. One half of it was presented to him for study, and quite a fine photographic copy of it appears in his admirable work on "Hawaiian Physical Formations," of which he made a critical study.

CHAPTER VI

MAKING THE TWELVE-INCH REFLECTOR

DURING the winter of 1877 we procured, through Heroy & Marrenner, of New York, glass disks for the reflecting telescope which we had decided to make after my first talk with Professor Langley. We decided to make it of as large diameter as we could handle in the little shop; so we fixed upon twelve inches as the maximum diameter of the glass. It was not difficult to procure the disks, nor were they very costly; so, fearing a repetition of my unfortunate accident in breaking one of the object-glass lenses, we ordered and received two very excellent disks.

A focal length of ten feet was decided upon, and the grinding and fining tool readily prepared for commencing the work. The emery was washed for the different grades, and the disks were cut out of the square plates — just how I cannot remember at this writing. So Ma and I commenced the work that was to take we did not know how long. It all had to be done after my daily work at the mill, and it would not, it could not have been done without the deep and abiding interest of my wife.

Our evenings were frequently interrupted by visitors who wanted to see the heavens in the five-inch telescope which was mounted in what was then the garret of our home, but I do not and did not regret the delay, so great was the pleasure of our visitors at seeing the moon, planets, star clusters, nebulæ, and occasionally a comet, in our telescope. But it required many months of labor before we had carried the work far enough along on the reflecting telescope mirror to do the polishing and testing.

Dr. Draper's splendid work, which had been loaned me by Professor Langley, gave full directions for testing the surface or curve of the mirror (Foucault method); and this was supplemented by letters from Dr. Draper himself with whom I had become acquainted by correspondence.

Unfortunately, I had no place where I could make these tests except the open space under the house, and this had to serve the purpose for the completion of the twelve-inch. After many nights of polishing, figuring, and testing, I concluded that the glass was as good as I could make it under the conditions of temperature changes that it had to undergo in working it in the little shop and testing it under the house. One of my greatest mistakes or blunders was that, owing perhaps to the limited time at my command each evening, I did not wait long enough after polishing to see the effects when the increased temperature caused by the polishing had subsided or distributed equally in the mass of the disk. This can be explained to the reader, unacquainted with the delicate methods employed in testing an accurate surface, in this way: if the warm hand were pressed upon such a surface as I am describing for, say, ten seconds, and if the glass was a few degrees cooler than the hand, a cameo of the hand would be raised on the surface. If then the surface were polished before the raised impression of the hand had subsided, this raised figure would be polished off; and then, when the glass would come to a normal temperature, there would be an intaglio or depressed figure of the hand, instead of the raised or cameo figure we had before. This fact is well known to all opticians who have to deal with accurate optical instruments.

But at last our twelve-inch was ready to receive its coat of silver. A splendid tube had been made ready for me by my young friend Edward Klages, a carpenter by trade; and I had made a pattern, and had a casting made, with a temporary though rather light equatorial mounting for it. This was set upon a brick foundation, and a platform built around it, so that observations could be made within our sky limits, which, unfortunately, were restricted in the south and southeast. Nevertheless, we had a fair portion of the sky at command, and were content.

There were several known methods for silvering front surfaces, but at the time my own knowledge of chemistry was limited, and I found that the chemist I consulted could give me but little information on silvering the front surfaces of glass, though quite a number of processes for silvering the inside of mirrors, like reflectors, looking-glasses, etc., were known. Dr. Draper's modification of the Cimeg Process was tried time and again; and as silver was a pretty costly affair for me, I was much discouraged, though at times I succeeded in getting a fair, but not satisfactory, surface of silver.

The mirror had already been tried on the moon with its unsilvered surface, and while its light value was only about one eighth of what it should be, the defining powers were very promising.

My attention had been called by an English friend in the Adams mould shop to a journal printed in London called the "English Mechanic and World of Science"; I borrowed a few numbers and found there a method of silvering by a process requiring heat. So my wife and I prepared to make a trial of the new process. I found everything in readiness when I came home from the mill; and after supper we went to the little shop where the water was soon warmed in the containing vessel by steam heat from the boiler, as rigorous cleanliness in all the processes had to be observed. We had poured the silver solution with its reducer to change it to the metallic form; and you can imagine our delight and joy when we saw a beautiful deposit of silver covering the surface.

But, alas, alas, our joy was soon turned to sorrow, to grief, to keen disappointment that never could be described in words, when we saw and heard our disk crack from edge to center! Not to this day have I determined the real cause of the disaster, although two causes might explain it: unequal heating of the mass of the glass (but this was done so carefully that the second explanation may be more satisfactory) or the possibility that a jet of cold air, coming through a crack in the side of the workshop and impinging upon one side of the glass, cooled it at one point, and hence the rupture.

I do not like to write about this second disappointment in our optical work when we appeared to be just at the climax of success; for this last failure seemed to affect me more than the first one. Failure after all these months, and just when we had reached the goal! What visions I had destroyed in a moment! One of them was the wonderful view I should have of the planet Mars, then coming into the best position for observing that it had been or would be in for years. It was the year 1877, when Professor Asaph Hall discovered the two satellites of the planet.

If I remember correctly, I slept little or none that night, though my dear wife tried her best to cheer me by saying we could finish another glass, as we had both the disk and the experience. I went to the mill the following morning; I walked around like a crazy man; I could not collect my thoughts or concentrate them upon anything. In fact, I think it would have been a Godsend if there had been a breakdown in the machinery that day to take my mind off that broken mirror.

About four o'clock in the afternoon I stopped and pondered for a moment, and this expression came from me, and could almost have been heard, I am sure, had there been any one near me: "What a fool you are, to worry this way; this worry will never mend that broken glass." I am not certain that I was a believer in telepathy then, or that I am now, but somehow I felt in my innermost soul that something was going on at home. I started home as early as possible that evening, and as I climbed the hill it was not with the same heavy heart that I had as I walked down it that morning. As I opened the door I was met with a smile and a kiss, and then dear Ma asked me to go out to the little shop before we sat down to supper. I thought possibly something unfortunate had happened out there. But instead, what did I see? The little shop in prime order, a fire burning under the boiler, engine oiled ready to start, and the extra disk in the lathe ready to have its edge turned with the diamond tool, and its surface roughed out to the approximate curve. Could any one have done more? The memory of that moment, filled with the love and confidence of the one who was more than life to me, I can never forget. To make a long story short, in about two months from that evening, in the early spring of 1878, the new twelve-inch mirror was ready to be silvered.

I had made quite a number of experiments with various methods of silvering by this time, and at last I found a method, or rather a modification of a method, which I had seen in the "Scientific American," called Burton's method, by which I succeeded in obtaining most admirable results in silvering mirrors on the front surface, although it was originally intended for back surfaces, looking-glasses, etc. So simple, so certain was this method, that I at once sent a communication to the "English Mechanic and World of Science," describing it in full for the benefit of my amateur friends of whom there were at that time, literally speaking, scores who were trying to make their own reflecting telescopes.

Little did I think at the time that this method would become *the* method, and be universally used for front-surface mirrors. The formula has been published in perhaps every chemical journal in the world; and although I am writing this note more than forty years after I had the pleasure of giving it to the world, without money and without price, I often have pleasant reminders of the value of my first humble contribution to the makers of reflecting telescopes.

Almost forty years later I stood in the laboratory of the Mount Wilson Observatory, admiring the beautiful silvered surface of the great one-hundred-inch reflecting telescope mirror, made by my old-time friend Professor Ritchey. Expressing my pleasure to him, he replied: "Well, it was silvered by Brashear's process." Many other methods have since been devised; but I know of none more certain and more easily applied. I think we silvered the surface of the great seventy-two-inch mirror for the Dominion Observatory at Victoria, British Columbia — made by Mr. McDowell at our workshops and finished in April, 1918 — in just about two hours and thirty minutes, including the operations of cleaning, mixing chemicals, and final polishing of the surface.

It can readily be seen from this description that there was no more experimenting on the new twelve-inch mirror; and, after a beautiful bright coat of silver was deposited upon its surface, and upon that of the small flat diagonal mirror for reflecting the beams from the central cone to the side of the tube, as in the Newtonian type of telescope, we were ready for the first clear night and our first look at the heavens.

I am not sure that I did not audibly express a soliloquy at the sight that met my eyes as I placed the telescope on the Star Cluster in Perseus, the Nebula in Andromeda, the binary star Albireo in Cygni! Not even the views in the thirteen-inch refractor at Allegheny could, to my mind, exceed in beauty the glorious views in the twelve-inch reflector. There was a reason for it too. Not that the glass Ma and I had made was better intrinsically than the Allegheny Observatory telescope, but because rays of light from these heavenly objects did not suffer from what is called residual chromatic aberration; or, in other words, all bright objects seen in a refractor are more or less colored; and much light is absorbed in passing through the glass lenses. Some light is lost by reflection in a silvered-glass telescope, but since there is no separation of light rays in the reflector, all bright objects are seen in their normal tints. Take for instance the binary star Albireo (Beta Cygni). Where one star of the system is orange yellow, the companion is a cerulean blue. With the gathered light of as large a glass as the twelve-inch, these two stars are pictures of beauty one can never forget — two brilliant diamonds, orange and blue, shining with their transcendent luster in that far-off setting in yonder blue sky! I shall never forget that first night with the twelve-inch which Ma and I enjoyed, not ourselves alone, but also our neighbors around us.

The twelve-inch reflector has had a useful life. For several years I used it for observation, making a study of many of the comets, the surface of Jupiter, and the floor of the crater Plato on the moon with it. I then loaned it to Professor Langley for a part of the apparatus with which he was making some important research at the Allegheny Observatory. Later on it was loaned to Professor Very, a former assistant of Professor Langley, who had gone to the observatory at Salem, Massachusetts; then to Professor Hale, and lastly loaned to Professor Very again, who had it in his possession for four or five years. After my old home and the workshop on the hill had been purchased by the good women of Pittsburgh for a Social Settlement, I had the good fortune to secure the mirror for the museum to be kept in the house, although Professor Very was quite loath to give it up, as it had aided him greatly in his astrophysical studies.

I cannot pass over this period of my struggles without stopping long enough to pay tribute to my good friend Dr. Henry Draper, who gave me some of my first words of encouragement. I had become acquainted with him through correspondence, as mentioned before, and he was never too busy to answer my letters in such a way as to help me solve the problems which were troubling me in the work I loved. His letters found me a toiler in the rolling mill, and together with his researches and his work on "The Construction of a Silvered-Glass Telescope and Its Use in Celestial Photography," they opened a new world, a new heaven to me, and I know I was only one of the many earnest toilers of science befriended by his great heart. Indeed, his book was of almost inestimable value to hundreds who were enabled to make their own instruments through a knowledge gained by studying it.

I find among my possessions a letter he wrote me in early February, 1878, which may give some idea of his sympathetic understanding and desire to help in my problems:

Your very interesting letter has come to hand and I am glad to hear from you and learn that you have had such success. Your improvements on the various processes are very ingenious and important. I can sympathize with you about cracking your mirror, for I lost one in almost exactly the same way.

You will find, no doubt, a considerable improvement in the action of your telescope by grinding and polishing a flat mirror. Most of the plate-glass one can buy is apt to be irregular locally and the image is much injured by it. By taking three disks of plate-glass and grinding one side of each of them alternately on the other two, you can get a flat surface. In making your polisher, use as hard a pitch as you can and polish one glass completely before polishing at the others. But use the others occasionally on the pitch tool to keep it flat. It is a difficult job to make a perfectly flat surface, but you can test it by the Foucault process by trying it in connection with your concave mirror; in other words, instead of putting the lamp and eyepiece in front of the mirror, put them at one side of the optical axis and direct the light by your flat mirror. You can then see what errors it gives to the beam of light from the concave mirror. On looking at a star with your telescope, if the flat mirror is slightly convex or concave the star will look like a small cross instead of a disk.

As to eye-pieces, it will probably be best for you to buy rather than make them. They are not expensive, but are troublesome to construct. You might use the eye-pieces or lenses of a microscope if you can get one. Stackpole and Brother of 49 Fulton Street, New York, can inform you where you can purchase them.

I have sent by this mail a pamphlet on my discovery of oxygen in the sun which I beg you to accept as a testimonial of esteem for your perseverance and well-directed labor. Please make my respects to your wife; such a partner is an invaluable assistant as I know from similar experience.

Very truly

HENRY DRAPER

After my good friend had passed over to the Summer Land, I had the pleasure of continuing my friendship with members of his distinguished family. In after years I went out to his old observatory at Hastings-on-the-Hudson, where I spent two grand, aye, glorious hours delving into the work of that famous workshop, two hours that will linger in my memory as long as life can last. No one outside the Draper family has ever visited that sacred spot that appreciated it, enjoyed it, drank in its reminiscences, its story of labor, toil, and anxious waiting for breaking clouds, more than I did. As I stood by the

noble sixteen-inch telescope and remembered the work
it had done in the first lunar photograph; when I remembered that it was the pioneer of so many hundreds of
telescopes of its kind that had gladdened the heart of the
struggling amateur; when I stood by the grand twenty-
eight-inch and thought of its maker and the blotting-out
of his noble life, I could not repress a tear of sorrow and
I asked myself the question, "Does death end all?"

CHAPTER VII
HOME AND FRIENDS

Now for a rest from the story of our shop labors to tell about the many visitors who came to our little home on the hill as the news spread abroad of the completion of the big glass. About this time various Chautauqua classes in Pittsburgh were hard at work studying astronomy without a telescope; and request after request came to me to give these classes an evening. How I managed to care for so many I cannot tell at this late day; but I am sure I am not overestimating when I say that at least a thousand people of all classes came to our house during the last five years of our stay on the South Side hills.

Among those who came to visit us and look in our telescope was my old and respected friend, Andrew Burt, at that time an honored Pittsburgh school teacher, and the author of "Burt's Grammar." He brought with him a coterie of teachers, all of whom enjoyed an evening with the stars, and, I am sure, carried away pleasant memories with them. One evening I remember well, when by invitation all the office force of the mill came to spend an evening with us. As I write these lines, not one of them is left on this "old round earth."

Busy as we were, we never denied the privilege of seeing the beauties of the heavens to any one, and although many, if not all of the older folks who came to us on the

South Side hills have gone over to the Summer Land, yet every now and then I meet some of the younger men of that day who tell me the story of how they had their first look at the heavens in our big telescope.

My readers will forgive me, I know, if I tell some of the funny things that happened at the home-made observatory on the hill. Sometimes I would have a nondescript who cared no more for the beauty of the heavens than I did to see a dog-fight who would persist in wanting to see the man in the moon, or to have proof that it was not made of green cheese. At other times folks entirely ignorant of astronomy would express their delight, and they were always helped to understand what they saw as much as their limited knowledge and my simplest explanation could help them.

One night I was alone rather late observing a telescopic comet. A man and his wife — she with a loaded market-basket — came along, stopped and looked over the fence. I invited them to come in and have a look at the moon, and they readily accepted the invitation. After looking at the moon for a few moments, the man said to his wife, "It just looks like Schweitzer cheese." She, however, had a different opinion, and said it looked like gold.

I then turned the telescope on the beautiful double star Mizar in the handle of the Big Dipper. The man admired it in his own quaint way, and then asked me to point out the other stars. I showed him the stars in the handle, and then the bowl, and told him it was called the Big Dipper. Gazing at it for a moment, he threw up his hands and exclaimed, "Mine Gott, mine friend, ich hab seen them same stars in Germany!"

There is another yarn I cannot resist telling. The young farmer who had been bringing Mrs. Brashear her supply of vegetables asked her one day if I would let him look in the big telescope if he came up some clear evening. She encouraged him to do so, and I found him waiting one night to see the sights. I did not know whether or not he had any knowledge of astronomy, but I asked him what he would like to look at. He replied, "Juniper." I told him that unfortunately that planet was not visible in the sky at the time. Then he expressed a desire to see "Satan." But his Satanic Majesty was not around either. The climax came when he asked if I could show him the "Star of Jerusalem!" I ended it by showing him the moon and some clusters, and he went home very happy.

I remember, too, an old gentleman over eighty years of age who climbed the hill one moonlight night for a look in the telescope. The good man was utterly exhausted when he reached the house, and Ma and I had him lie down on the lounge to rest before climbing the stairs to the telescope. The views that night were fine, and I can hear the soliloquy yet of the dear fellow as he said, "For many years I have desired to see the beauties of the heavens in a telescope. I have read about them and heard lectures about them, but I never dreamed they were so beautiful." We invited him to stay all night; but as it was moonlight, and much easier for him to go down the hill than to come up, he insisted on going home. I went part of the way with him to see that he got along all right; and all the way he expressed his delight at having the wish of a lifetime gratified that night.

Three weeks later the funeral cortège of that old man

passed along the road on the opposite hillside that led to the cemetery, and it has always been a pleasure to remember that I was able to be of some service in gratifying one of his desires of a lifetime.

I think that all my life I have been partial to old people and children, and it has always been a source of genuine pleasure to contribute to their happiness. I used to have a half-dozen poor ragged urchins around me at one time making observations with the twelve-inch. Not a boy of them would touch it, and if any of the boys that knew me would see another boy doing damage, there would be a row at once. My shop was never locked, day or night, except when we were away, and with all those boys constantly in and out I never lost a tool, not even a hammer.

As I look back over this period of my life I realize more than ever that I can never overestimate the value of the helping hand, the devotion and self-sacrifice of my wife. Any little success I may have attained either in my mechanical or purely scientific work, I owe in large measure to her. The right word at the right time and a helping hand at the critical moment have saved most of us from defeat and won for us great victories.

Night after night I came home from the rolling mill to find steam up and everything in readiness for work in the little shop. Ma kept the engine oiled, the tools and bottles in order, and the room neat and clean. After supper was over and the dishes washed, she would come back to help me in my mechanical work and later in my observations. Her material assistance was valuable, but the inspiration I had from her which helped me over the rough places of life to the next step is completely beyond my poor words of appreciation. She was a helpmate in the fullest sense of that significant word.

I know she found the work congenial; but not only did she do everything possible for its success, but what was even more to me, she made our home happy for ourselves and for all who came to our little cottage on the hill. I do not remember that we had a real dining-room, so our dining-room was the kitchen as well, and before we left that house (1886) many noted men dined with us there, and Ma always had something good to eat.

Professor E. E. Barnard, of the Yerkes Observatory, wrote me a few years ago on the occasion of my seventy-fifth birthday anniversary (1915) recalling his first visit to our home:

I had wandered forth for the first time from my native town in search of science and scientific men, and had finally come to Pittsburgh in my wanderings.

I had just arrived on a very early morning train, on which I had neither dined nor slept, for the diner and sleeper had been a special terror to me in all this journey. After a vaguely directed search I finally found myself on an unpaved road cut in the clay soil of a steep hillside, hunting for Number 3 Holt Street (this street and number have remained in my memory all these years), a street that seemed to have no existence in the memory of any one I had met.

A man passed by with his dinner bucket — and this shows how early I was abroad that morning, and how hungry I was to notice the man's dinner bucket, which at that moment, could I have had my way without bloodshed, would have become a "breakfast" bucket. This man said he didn't know of any street by that name. When I asked him, however, if he knew where John A. Brashear lived, he said, "Why, he lives right there in that house," pointing to a small cottage not fifty feet away, at the side of the road. "Then," said I, "this must be Holt Street, and that house must be Number 3." I felt then that it was a mighty fine thing to be a man who was better known than the street he lived on!

The warm greeting that met me in that small cottage lingers in my memory with a freshness that time cannot wither. The good woman who asked "Have you had any breakfast?" is dead now and she is mourned by thousands, but when she died there was no sincerer mourner than the young man who had met her for the first time that morning. The admission on my part that I hadn't had anything to eat since the previous morning was taken instantly as a challenge, and soon a delicious breakfast of ham and eggs and coffee — and such biscuit! — greeted my appreciative soul. . . .

This, dear Brashear, is one of the many, many reasons I have to regret that I cannot sit down with you and your friends this day and enjoy another meal, which, however grand it might be, could never approach in sweetness that early morning meal of a third of a century ago!

So it was with all who came in contact with Ma. Prince or pauper, rich or poor, all who were worthy were recipients of her kindness.

I cannot tell at this date how I ever found time to continue my work and my studies when I remember the hundreds of visitors who came to us, but I never could see the pleasure or joy in not sharing the beautiful things in life with all who loved them. I have never forgotten the days of my boyhood when I had no sled and some other fellow asked me to "get on behind." So in order to share with more people the results of my work and observations, I formed the habit of contributing to the newspapers short articles on the planets, moon, comets, etc. I read every day while on the cars going to and from the mill, and oftentimes, as has been said before, late into the night. But my writing had all to be done at home and sandwiched in between visitors. I managed to find time for this somehow, and by 1880 I had contributed articles which were published in the "Evening Chronicle," the "Ledger," "Dispatch," and "Commercial Gazette" of Pittsburgh, and the "Alleghenian."

It is never possible to tell which acts of ours may reap fruitful results in later years. It was these articles, written gratuitously for the pleasure and help of my fellow beings who were interested in the stars, that helped to introduce me to the man who was to be my benefactor throughout his life.

CHAPTER VIII

GOING INTO BUSINESS FOR MYSELF

Now that we had succeeded in making a fair reflecting telescope for our own use and for that of our friends, the question came to me: Will it be worth while to try to make them for others? It was my idea to make only the optical parts, but to furnish the drawings too, so that amateurs could construct their own mountings. I had been doing odd jobs for Professor Langley ever since my first visit to the Allegheny Observatory, and I had helped a friend make a reflector of about six inches aperture. I concluded to try my hand at further work of this nature, so I placed an advertisement in the "Scientific American" which, as I remember, read about this way:

Silvered-glass specula, diagonals
and eye-pieces made for amateurs desiring to
construct their own telescopes. Address

John A. Brashear,
No. 3 Holt Street,
South Side, Pittsburgh, Pa.

Alas for me! Hundreds of inquiries came to me from that advertisement. I had no clerk, and I was still hard at work in the rolling mill — up early in the morning, home after six. How was I to answer those scores of letters? And how make specula for the fellows who wanted them?

However, Ma and I worked diligently at them every hour we could spare, except Saturday night. That night for several years was spent with my friend, Dr. William Herron of Allegheny, who had a fine four-inch Browning telescope mounted on the roof of his house. He also had a splendid Browning spectroscope which I had the privilege of using many nights, and which he loaned to Professor Langley, as the Observatory did not at that time possess one. The doctor and I became inseparable friends.

Ma and I continued this day and night work, which we began when I first started my five-inch lens in 1872, until 1881. Then one evening Dr. Herron on one of his visits found me laid up in bed, a pretty sick man who did not know what was the matter with him. The doctor at once pronounced it a nervous breakdown from overwork. I was a comparatively young man then, but it was three weeks before I dared go to work again, and when I did go back, I had to go very slowly. Dr. Herron watched me carefully, and soon issued warning that I must, in common parlance, "let up" with caring for the machinery of the rolling mill and making optical instruments besides.

Ma and I had a long talk one evening as to what we should do. I had saved about three hundred dollars besides having made payments on the lots we had purchased and the lumber we had bought; but we still were in debt about eight hundred dollars. If I gave up my work at the mill, could we earn enough by our optical work to make both ends meet? We were wedded to the business of making astronomical telescopes and believed there was a field for it in America if we could only hold out till the time when we could make it pay.

Our daughter Effie had been married in March, 1880, to a young man, James B. McDowell, who was employed in the glass works of the Bryce Company. From his first visit to our home I had noticed he was considerably interested in the work in which I was engaged, and from the beginning it was apparent that he had a peculiar genius for the work. To bring this part of the story to a climax, it was decided at our family councils (Effie and Jimmie were living with us at the time) that I should quit the rolling mill and do my utmost to succeed in our chosen pursuit, pooling my meager income with Jimmie's to tide us over until our business was on a paying basis. It was surely an epoch in our life-history, and I am a little afraid that failure would have been our lot had not the Good Samaritan William Thaw found us just at this turning-point in our lives.

After I had fully recovered from the illness just mentioned, about July, 1881, Professor Langley sent me a letter asking if I would come over to the Observatory, as he wanted to see me on an important matter in connection with his proposed trip to Mount Whitney, Colorado, where he was to make a further study of the selective absorption of the earth's atmosphere and also to make an effort to see the solar corona, independently of a total solar eclipse, in the transparent and dustless atmosphere of the mountain height. I learned that he wanted me to silver his heliostat mirror with the most perfect coat of silver possible, so as to show no microscopic scratches on the surface, in order that no diffused light should be reflected into his observing telescope when viewing the reflected image of the sun.

I carried the mirror home with me — it was one that had been made by the Clarks — and succeeded in getting an exquisitely beautiful surface upon it, showing no blemishes except the few left in the polishing and figuring of the glass surface. Wrapping it up carefully, the surface covered with absorbent cotton, I carried it over to the Observatory early one evening; and as it was in the early summer, it was quite light when I reached the top of the hill. I saw a gentleman sitting on the Observatory steps talking with Professor Langley, so I kept myself in the background until Professor Langley saw me and called me to him. He insisted on opening the package to look at the surface without going into the Observatory, although I put in a protest at exposing it to the night air. He expressed great satisfaction and thanks for the beautiful surface; and then introduced me to his friend sitting by his side, who was apparently as eager to see the silvered mirror as Langley was.

Who should this be but the great philanthropist William Thaw, the friend of science, the friend of education, the friend of the struggling artist, musician, and student, friend of the University, friend and promoter of all scientific work at the Observatory. I had heard of him many times, but had never met him. He asked me at once if I was the young man who wrote the articles on comets, etc., for the "Evening Chronicle." I had to say "Yes" to his questions.

"Young man, I want to know you better. Come over to my house to-morrow night and let us have a talk together," said he.

I did not have the remotest idea of what he wanted;

but, of course, I said I would be there. I had purchased a copy of the "Scientific American" on my way to the Observatory, probably had taken it with me to read on the cars, as I never wasted the hours on the cars without something of value to read or study. Taking the paper out of my pocket, he wrote the directions of how I should find him; and the margin of that paper on which he wrote those directions I have to this day.

By this time the twilight had well-nigh disappeared, and I asked Professor Langley if he had seen the new comet. He had not, and Mr. Thaw expressed a desire to have a view of it in the telescope. Professor Langley asked me if I could locate it. It was at that time invisible to the naked eye. I thought I could do so; and it was not long until we had the big telescope set on the stranger. I left early, and all the way home that night I wondered what Mr. Thaw wanted with me.

On the following night I found him awaiting me in the modest parlor of his house; and as he was tired after his day's work at the railroad office (he was at that time one of the vice-presidents of the Pennsylvania Railroad Lines West of Pittsburgh), he was lying on the lounge. He asked me to be seated, and, with his pointed queries, learned the general outline of my life-history from my birth to the day I met him.

Then he bade me good-night, saying, "To-morrow night I am coming over to see you." I told him it would be difficult for him to find his way up our hill on account of the steep and miserable road; but he said he would come early enough so that Michael, his driver, could easily find the way.

However, it was dark when he reached our home the following night; and as there were some unexpected visitors looking at the heavens, he tarried at the platform for a short time while I was showing them the binary star Albireo. Expressing a desire to see the object we were observing, he climbed the ladder to the eye-piece, and I well remember his expression, "I have never seen anything so beautiful in all my life!" and he had seen many things of beauty in the heavens in the telescope at the Observatory, as well as in a portable instrument of his own. Leaving the telescope in the hands of a young friend who occasionally assisted me when visitors came, I walked with Mr. Thaw down the path to the little shop, which was in perfect order, as it always was in those days when Ma cared for it. He looked around for a few minutes and then expressed a desire to visit in our home. Here he met my wife, and the partner in our business; and after chatting awhile, he left. Before bidding us good-night, he took us both by the hands, and said: "I see you have the boat, the captain and the pilot, and now what you want is some water to float the vessel in. You must have a better and larger workshop, better machinery, better equipment. Study out your plans, then come to see me as soon as you can. Good-night."

After he had left us we talked and talked long before we went to our rest that night. We did not comprehend his meaning. Was he to loan us the money to do this? If so, what would our chances be of ever paying it back again? However, the next day and for several days, I was at work on a very modest plan, in order to carry out Mr. Thaw's instructions. I planned a building, twelve feet by twenty feet, with engine, boiler, two lathes, a drill press, better grinding and polishing machine, etc., and a few days later I made a report to Mr. Thaw. He expressed himself as well satisfied with my plans, and at once wrote me a check for three thousand dollars to pay for the materials.

I asked him when and how he expected me to pay the money back again, telling him I feared debt, and was much concerned over the uncertainty of paying it back. He told me it was his privilege to do this for me in the interest of a science we both loved so well; and since I was loath to accept the money as a gift, he let me down easy by saying if I ever became wealthy I could either return it to him or pass it on to the other fellow! Moreover, he at once proposed to take another burden off my mind by paying all the indebtedness on our home, which was done.

As soon as the matter was settled between Mr. Thaw and myself as to the new equipment, a contract was made with an old neighbor, Mr. Davis, for the building; and by the time it was finished, the machinery was in readiness to be placed. I can well remember what a job it was to get the six-horse-power engine and boiler up that steep hill. Another item a little out of the line of such matters: There were four men, including their boss, who brought that engine up the hill. It was one o'clock when they had it unloaded. My wife said, "Pa, those men must be hungry after this big job. I am going to cook some oysters, and I have plenty of other things. As soon as they are ready, bring them in." My, but those fellows were hungry, and how they did eat! I was mortally afraid there wouldn't be enough for them, but Ma was equal to the demand and those men never forgot her thoughtful kindness.

December, 1881, found us with the machinery installed in the new shop, ready to put full-time work on the orders we had secured both through Professor Langley and the single advertisement in the "Scientific American." Just a year before, on Christmas Eve of 1880, I had made the following entry in my diary:

Shipped the three mirrors I had made by Adams Express today. One to Hunt, C.O.D. $59.50; one to Hesse, $23.50; one to Bishop, $35. These are my first actual shipments and *I do hope they will turn out good.*

It had been my ideal in all my work to *make it turn out good,* as good as my ability and efforts could make it, and regardless of the time it took. It was this desire for perfection that made my work valuable to scientists, but, coupled with a lack of interest in what it cost me in time and money to do my work, it led me from this time on into frequent financial worries. Without Mr. Thaw's aid I fear it would have been impossible for me to keep on.

CHAPTER IX

THE ROWLAND DIFFRACTION GRATINGS

THE shops finished, orders began to come in that I found impossible to fill all by myself. Arrangements were made to have a mechanic come to do the instrumental part of the work — George Klages, who had learned his trade in a brass foundry and machine shop. It was not long before young McDowell gave up his position at the glass works to join us, and his knowledge of the art of glass-making was an invaluable aid.

He soon took hold with an ambition to do his best, and his best was excellent. Klages took hold of the instrumental part under my direction. One of the first pieces of apparatus made in the machine or instrument shop was one I have always designated as a solar-energy storage box. The order for this was given to us by Professor Langley, who at the time was making his classic research on the radiant energy of the sun. It was too large in diameter to be turned in our largest lathe, but the head was raised, as my mechanical friends will understand, and the job finished to Langley's satisfaction.

He used this apparatus with success in his experiments. His results as determined in those early experiments may be summed up in this little paragraph copied from his work "The New Astronomy," many of the pages of which he read to me before they were sent to the printer:

"If the entire heat of the sun was concentrated on a column of ice fifteen miles in diameter, and reaching from the earth to the moon, a distance of two hundred and forty thousand miles, it would be melted and dissipated into vapor in one second of time."

Just about this time, when we were making some silvered-glass specula for reflecting telescopes, we had a letter from Dr. Charles S. Hastings, then Professor of Physics at Johns Hopkins University, asking us to polish for him a prism of some glass that was taken or cut from one of the disks made for the Lick telescope objective. Mr. McDowell did this piece of work for him so well that Hastings called it to the attention of Professor Henry A. Rowland, his chief, and one of America's most distinguished physicists. Now Rowland, who was interested in the wave-length analysis of the solar spectrum, had worked out a theory of concave and plane gratings, which are simply a series of fine parallel lines drawn very close to each other on an accurately formed surface, plane or curved. He had with great ingenuity and skill designed and constructed a machine for ruling these lines, with an accuracy far beyond anything that had been done before. This ruling engine had been installed in an underground vault in order that it might not be disturbed in its delicate work by vibrations due to street traffic, and also to secure as nearly a constant temperature as was possible. Prior to the introduction of the gratings ruled by this machine, prism spectroscopes, in most cases of low dispersion, were almost invariably employed in spectroscopic work. Rutherfurd had ruled some fairly good gratings, but very few of them were available and these were of small size.

Hence the invention of Rowland's ruling engine was of great importance to the scientific world.

The success of the ruling engine, however, depended on the geometrical perfection of the surfaces of the speculum-metal plates to be ruled. They required not only a very high polish, but a very accurate surface; say, no error of one fifth of a light wave, or approximately, one two-hundred-thousandth of an inch.

Professor Rowland, on seeing the work McDowell had done for Dr. Hastings in polishing the glass prism, at once asked us to polish and correct some plates for him. We accepted the order, but found we had undertaken a task that proved well-nigh capable of flooring us. Speculum-metal polishing was a lost art; at least, our ideal of it. However, McDowell at last mastered the business of giving the surfaces an exquisitely beautiful polish and a "figure," as we call the accurate surface, that left nothing to be desired. The finished plates were sent to Rowland, and his verdict awaited with great anxiety.

Professor Langley was at Johns Hopkins University at the time, giving a course of lectures. He wrote us a letter, saying he had been with Professor Rowland all the afternoon, testing and witnessing the test of the gratings ruled on our plates by Rowland. After saying that they had satisfied his most critical requirements, he added, "If you have thus satisfied Rowland, you need not be afraid to work for any scientific man in the world." Of course, we looked anxiously for a letter from Rowland himself. It came, and it not only expressed satisfaction at our work, but took up the matter of a business arrangement for supplying these gratings to scientists. We were to furnish the plates, Rowland was to rule them and send them back to us, and we were to act as distributing agents for them.

This — and I may call it a crisis in our early venture — opened a new field for us, and not among amateurs, but among the most advanced scientific men of the day. The simplicity and convenience of the Rowland Grating, combined with its high dispersion and perfect adaptation for photography, had a revolutionary effect wherever it was introduced. It raised spectroscopy from the qualitative to the quantitative stage, and for years was a prize sought by every physical laboratory in the world. It was of immense service to a large class of scientific investigators, and for years Rowland's activities, thoughts, and interests were centered around the famous ruling engine, the product of which had enabled him to achieve one of the most brilliant investigations of his period.

Several thousand of these plates were made at our shops and distributed over the world. Previous to 1900 we supplied large-size concave grating spectroscopes to the West Point Military Academy, the Sloane Physical Laboratory, the Royal University of Ireland at Dublin, Cambridge University in England, the University of Turin in Italy, McGill University in Canada, and Paris University in France. The following incident may reveal their peculiar interest in the scientific world.

In 1884, Lord Kelvin, then Sir William Thomson, gave a course of very remarkable lectures at Johns Hopkins University to a small and select audience made up of professors of mathematics and physics from numerous colleges and universities who had been invited to attend by the president and faculty of Johns Hopkins. There were twenty-one in all, and at the conclusion of the course they wanted to present to Lord Kelvin some testimonial of appreciation of the lectures. For this they selected a large Rowland Grating, specially prepared and ruled for the purpose. In my friendship with Lord Kelvin I found him devoted to his science and ready to help his fellow scientist.

My relations with Professor Rowland lasted for many years, and never but once did we have any differences, but that single experience gave me a comprehension of his great mind that possibly I could not have measured otherwise. He had been testing some of our grating plates with one of the test plates or planes that were made for him by Steinheil of Munich and found they were uniformly depressed in the center. He wrote me at once about the trouble, and I was much worried, for our tests showed them to be as perfect as we could make them.

I started at once for Baltimore and found Rowland at the laboratory when I reached the university. He immediately said to me, "Those last plates you made are all bad." I told him that was what brought me to Baltimore. We went into the room, set up the testing apparatus, and, sure enough, every plate showed a depression of half a wave length near the center. Professor Hastings who was present at the test remarked, "May not the error be in the test plane?" Professor Rowland said, "No, Steinheil makes the best planes in the world."

Fortunately, Hastings asked him if he did not have a mate to the plane made by Steinheil, and he remembered that he had. It was soon produced. The two test planes were put together, and lo, the error was doubled. Rowland showed his bigness right there. He "took it all back," as the boys say, and from that day on he never even tested another plate made by us.

An incident here will be worth recording. When my friend Professor Keeler, of the Allegheny Observatory, went over to Germany to study under Quincke and others (Mr. Thaw had furnished the means for this purpose), he took with him a three-inch grating that had been given him by Professor Rowland. At the time, the largest gratings that had been made in Germany were those ruled by Nobert, whom microscopists will remember by his making of test bands for microscopic study. These gratings, if I remember correctly, were not over two centimeters on the ruled portion, less than one inch. When the learned German professor was lecturing to the students, he showed them one of Nobert's gratings with pride, saying it was one of the largest and most perfect gratings in existence. Keeler had the temerity to say that he had a grating three times as large as the Nobert grating, but the professor insisted that if he had one that size it was worthless. Keeler at once went to his dormitory, got the grating, and had the professor test it, who was astonished with its apparent beauty. His skepticism turned to unstinted praise.

An interesting controversy between Rowland and the English physicist Glazebrook occurred when the Rowland Gratings were beginning to be used. Glazebrook argued that concave gratings could not be used for precision work. The world of science knows to-day who won out in the controversy; and Glazebrook was a worthy adversary, a man who stands high among his compeers, and who has done great and good work in his chosen field.

As I write this note more than thirty-five years later, we are still making those beautiful plates and distributing them to institutions of learning all over the world. Rowland has passed on and his ashes lie in a niche in the stone wall of the ruling-engine vault, but this one of his notable inventions has probably done more to open new fields, and make possible greater discoveries in the domain of terrestrial, solar, and stellar physics — especially in the realm of spectrum analysis — than any other invention, not excluding the telescope itself. Marvelous discoveries have been made during the life-history of the diffraction grating, and the end is not yet.[1]

[1] Rowland died on April 16, 1901. A meeting in commemoration of his life and work was held at Baltimore, in the lecture room of the physical laboratory of Johns Hopkins University on October 26th of the same year. At the invitation of the president and faculty of the university, I gave the commemoration address on that occasion; and half an hour before the time set for this, a small group of Rowland's closest friends and associates were taken to the ruling-engine vault to witness an interesting event. They were Dr. D. C. Gilman, Dr. Ira Remsen, Dr. George F. Barker, Dr. J. S. Ames, Professor S. W. Stratton, John A. Brashear, and myself. The ashes of our friend enclosed in a bronze casket were, in accordance with his own desire, entombed in a niche in the stone wall of the vault, and the opening of the niche was sealed. The ceremony was simple but impressive, the more so because of the immediate presence of the beautiful piece of mechanism of which he was always so justly proud. To Brashear, who had been so intimately associated with both the engine and its creator, the occasion was one of strong though restrained emotion. (*Letter from Dr. T. C. Mendenhall.*)

CHAPTER X

ROCK–SALT PRISMS AND OTHER WORK

ONE of the easier of the earlier problems put into my hands was the polishing of rock-salt lenses and prisms. Tyndall had called the attention of the scientific world to the fact that pure rock salt was transparent to the long radiations or waves from the sun; and Professor Langley, having conceived the idea that he could study these radiations with reference to organic life upon the earth, invented an instrument which he called a spectrobolometer. The bolometer was a wonderful invention by which heat radiations of less than one-hundred-thousandth of a degree could be detected. To use this successfully in the problems that he had placed before him, it was necessary for him to have accurate lenses and prisms made of rock salt. A few rock-salt prisms had been made for him by Hoffman, of Paris, but the surfaces were not optically perfect enough to show more than the leading Fraunhofer lines. As rock-salt surfaces rapidly deteriorated from moisture, Professor Langley would frequently get his prisms from Paris with the surfaces totally ruined on account of the deliquescent nature of the salt, although they were supposed to be sent in hermetically sealed vessels; and sometimes, if they were all right, but were taken out on a damp day, the surfaces would soon go to pieces. Then he had to send them back to Paris for repolishing, and the result was that his investigations were greatly hindered because the prisms were so long in transit.

Mr. George Clark, of the Alvan Clark Company, succeeded in making one very excellent prism for Professor Langley, but never wanted to undertake any further work in this line. In Professor Langley's anxiety to carry on this interesting research, he asked me to undertake to polish the lenses and prisms, and see what I could do. I worked four or five weeks trying to make a perfect optical surface and get it to the Observatory in good condition; but failed time after time. I had been working all of one day and had given it up for a time, tired and weary. I wakened early the next morning, and an idea came to my mind as to how to master the problem. I could scarcely wait until after breakfast to try the method. It was eminently successful; and Langley gave me great praise for the result, for instead of being able to see only a few of the Fraunhofer lines, he could easily detect the nickel line between the two sodium lines of the spectrum. As Mr. McDowell later on managed to master the surfaces by the same process, I presume those surfaces and lenses were polished more than a hundred times during the classical research of Professor Langley on the infrared end of the spectrum. The frequent repolishing was, of course, necessitated by the affinity of the salt for the water vapor almost always present in the atmosphere; or, in other words, the deliquescent nature of salt.

At that time salt crystals were very hard to procure, but Dr. Hastings had presented Professor Langley with a very pure crystal, from which we made a lens and a prism about two and one fourth inches on the surfaces. Much later, in 1893, while going through the Russian Exhibit at the World's Fair in Chicago, I discovered several magnificent crystals of large size. I immediately telegraphed about them to Professor Langley, who was then at the Smithsonian Institution. He had no trouble, as a government official, in securing these beautiful and extraordinary crystals after the Exhibition was over. From one of these crystals we made a five-inch lens and a five by seven sixty-degree prism — something unheard of heretofore as to their dimensions — with which the researches of Langley were continued. They were so successful that they now form one of the most interesting and valuable researches ever made in physical science.

Langley was generous in his praise of my work with the rock-salt surfaces. At the Ann Arbor meeting of the American Association for the Advancement of Science, in 1885, he read a paper on "Some Hitherto Unmeasured Wave Lengths," in which he paid me such a compliment for my part in his work that I really felt ashamed and wished I were out of the place. He said that much of his success was due to my critical work on the rock-salt prisms which I worked for him and which were infinitely superior to any he could possibly obtain in Europe, and while those he got from Paris failed to show the ordinary Fraunhofer lines, the prisms I worked for him would show the *nickel* line between the D lines, and other lines correspondingly well, away up into the violet. I was greatly embarrassed by his praise, especially since my paper on "A Practical Method of Producing Accurate Rock-Salt

Surfaces for Optical Purposes" followed his remarks about me. The result was that I was proposed for a fellowship by no less than three sections, and I could not say a word, for I was unanimously elected. Of course it meant more work in the domain of research of a practical nature, and I believe I took the election without a grain of conceit, for I could not feel myself worthy of the honor.

This was not the first time I had read a paper before the American Association for the Advancement of Science. The year before I had attended the Philadelphia meeting, and I well remember that visit. We had invented and successfully used for several years a method of correcting the local errors in optical surfaces which proved to be very efficient, so much so that Professor Langley asked me to read a paper on the subject before the Philadelphia meeting in 1884.

I went, my mother and my wife accompanying me; and I well remember the moment when I was asked to get up and read my paper. How I trembled before those savants who had gathered there! Among them I remember Professor Newcomb, Professor Harkness, Professor Young, and others. That year the British Association had come over to hold their meeting at Montreal. After their sessions, many of them came down to Philadelphia to attend the meeting of the American Association. In the section where I read my paper there were several of the learned men of the British Association. After I had finished, a member of the British Association got up and made a most severe criticism of my paper, saying how much better and easier they made lenses and mirrors in England. It almost frightened the life out of me, but Professor C. A. Young came to my rescue and informed the gentleman that my paper was on the correction of lenses for astronomical purposes, requiring the greatest possible precision; while the gentleman who had made the criticism was talking about lighthouse lenses, which any amateur could grind and polish without the necessity of testing. Fortunately, my paper was published in full, with all the illustrations that had been made, in the annual volume of the Association for that year.

This method of correcting optical surfaces has been used since by many of the best opticians of the world; and is the method which, modified according to the character of the surface, was used by McDowell and his associate Frederick Hageman in the final correction of the great seventy-two-inch mirror recently made for the Canadian Dominion Observatory at Victoria, British Columbia.

I continued to attend these meetings as often as I could. Mr. Thaw, who was contributing financially so as to make it possible for me to continue my work, was eager for me to take advantage of opportunities to come in touch with the leading scientists of the day, and oftentimes provided me with railroad passes for meetings which were valuable. I remember the 1886 meeting of the Association where I upset my stomach because I listened to the pleadings of a half-dozen of the fair sex — Eves, I mean — and ate food which I had forsworn at the Philadelphia and Ann Arbor meetings, and then got a fearful cold besides. But I met many of the savants that year — Gould, Mendenhall, Gibbs, Newton, Brackett, Paul, Frisby, Harkness,

Brooks, and Barnard, and a host of other good fellows. I found them kind, considerate, interested in my work, and ready to lend a helping hand.

I was agreeably surprised to find that year that some ideas I gave in regard to studies in stellar photometry were considered new contributions to the subject, and of considerable weight. I contributed two papers which were well received. The fact is they did not receive an adverse criticism. One was on our new instrument for parallel work which did away with the personal equation and expedited the work very much. We called it a "Gravity Parallelometer." The other paper was on "Natural Gas in Reference to Its Utilization in Vertical Boilers." I was just beginning to realize then what a wonderful fuel natural gas was for optical work — so cheap, so handy, so little trouble, so safe and free from dust. It made the prettiest sodium flame for testing speculum plates, and it could be regulated in the morning for all day. I wished I could share it with everybody interested in optical work.

Another invaluable aid to our work at this time came from Dr. Charles S. Hastings, who later (1887) joined the Brashear Company. Dr. Hastings had calculated the curves of a six-inch refractor and a nine-inch one, now in the Observatory of the Johns Hopkins University. He proposed to join forces with us and calculate the curves of any objectives for which we might receive orders. He was a master in his line, and we were not up in the mathematics of optics; so we readily accepted his proposition, which proved to be one of the greatest and most important factors in our humble success. To his masterly knowledge of mathematical optics, with the added skill of Mr. McDowell and his boys in the shop, is due the successful making of perhaps half a hundred of the larger telescope objectives. We have made from, say, six-inch aperture to the thirty-inch, which is in our Allegheny Observatory, and the seventy-two-inch in the Canadian Dominion Observatory; and of all the large and small objectives which Dr. Hastings has computed, not one has failed to come up to the requirements.

The layman can perhaps readily understand the difficulties involved in such work when it is stated that no two pieces of glass — at least, made at different meltings — are exactly alike in their physical nature; and as we have had orders to make objectives corrected to ever so many different parts of the spectrum, and to consist of special kinds of glass, empiricism or guesswork has no place in their construction. To this day Dr. Hastings has remained our faithful advisor in all the difficult problems which have been brought before us.

One of the nice pieces of work made about this time was an aurora spectroscope for Professor Edward S. Holden. It was provided with a single carbon-bisulphide prism. I made an improvement in the frame holding the glass faces of the prism, by making the base of very thin brass, so that the expansion of the liquid would not injure the definition by distorting the glass faces, nor force open the peculiar cement used to attach them to the frame. Every one who has handled carbon bisulphide knows that its vapor is not as fragrant as a rose.

An eight-and-one-half-inch reflecting telescope was ordered and made for Norman Snow, whose son "Benny" has made a good name for himself in physical science, as well as his daughter Julia. A twelve-inch was made for Francis G. du Pont, the powder manufacturer of Wilmington. A great many specula were made, furnished with cells, and innumerable sketches made for the amateur so that he could construct his own telescope. We never neglected the requests from amateurs.

CHAPTER XI
THE NEW SHOPS AND WILLIAM THAW

An unpleasant and unfortunate episode comes in about here. We had made a fine mounting and speculum for a twelve-inch reflecting telescope, and we wanted to have a photograph taken of it. A friend, an amateur photographer, had sent his camera, and intended coming the day after to take the pictures for us. An unfortunate natural-gas explosion occurred the night before he was to come, and part of his drug-store had been wrecked; so he sent word to me to take the picture, as he had arranged everything except putting up the screen and exposing the plates. I undertook to put up the screen for a background, climbing up a ladder to do so. While putting in a nail, the ladder slipped, and I fell with my breast on a lathe, breaking four ribs and driving one of them into my lung. It was cold weather (February 3, 1885) and the shop had become overheated, so the door had been opened to cool it off. Somehow in my delirium I managed to get up, rush to the door for air, and fall out on the hard frozen ground, further injuring me.

A doctor was summoned, pronounced me in bad shape, placed many feet of surgeon's plaster around me, and I was put to bed, where I stayed for six weeks. It was a terrific shock, but my constitution, hardened by twenty-one years in the rolling mill, was able to withstand it.

At last I got out again and into the workshop; and although it was many a day before I could do anything, it was a joy to be with the boys again.

While I was suffering from the injury, Professor Langley and Mr. Thaw, who had heard of my accident, came to see me, Mr. Thaw slipping a goodly bank-note into Ma's hands with the admonition to leave nothing undone for my comfort. I felt the effects of that injury for a good many years, and even now, when I get "a little out of sorts," I feel the effects of an adhesion of one of my broken ribs to my left side. But then, any half-optimist would say, "It might have been worse."

Now that I have taken time to tell one of the more personal incidents of the eighties, I will follow it with another incident of which I am reminded here and which gives an idea of the difficulties of those days. We had had to depend upon cistern water for the house and shop up to this time; and often, when it was about used up, we had only one recourse — to shovel snow into it when a snowstorm came along; but I do not remember having to stop our work for lack of something in the way of water to fill our little boiler. The South Side waterworks had only recently laid a line over the top of the hill, which was supplied from a tank into which water was pumped from the waterworks below. We concluded to lay a line of pipe for ourselves. This we did by dint of hard work, hiring some help. One good fellow who lived on our hill dug some of the trench, got mad at some trivial thing, and for spite shoveled all the earth back again. I forget how we made friends with him again, but, as he was a sort of preacher, we won him over and he helped us finish the job.

After this we were troubled only once for want of a water supply while we were on the South Side hills. That was when the water was frozen in a portion of the line. I well remember one winter when a snowstorm almost buried us on the hill. These troubles were incidents and hardly worth telling, but that it took spunk and patience to fight them through goes without saying.

The work done in our shop had become so well known both in Europe and America that from time to time we had men of science visit us. Among them I recall Professor William A. Rogers, a well-known astronomer and physicist, and an inventor of several instruments of precision, including a ruling engine for dividing standard scales or measuring instruments. He investigated standards of measuring instruments in England and France and our own replicas of the standard yard and meter.

Professor Rogers had asked us to make some half-meter bars for him to copy the standards upon. They were to be made of speculum metal, and were not only to be highly polished on one surface, but made straight from end to end. I think the deviation from straightness was not to be over one-fifty-thousandth of an inch. I devised a machine to do this work, which in the skillful hands of McDowell produced some splendid results. Shorter bars were also made, on which Rogers ruled tenths of a millimeter, millimeters, and tenths of an inch, up to four inches. One of these bars he presented to me; and later on I gave it to the Brown & Sharpe Company, who have a most interesting collection of standards. These people were very kind to me through one of their splendid men; and I thought Rogers's standard would be safe in their hands. Few men that I have known were more devoted to science than Professor Rogers. He ruled a number of diffraction gratings, but he did not reach his ideal. My own opinion is that the lines and spaces were accurate enough, but, as Professor Rowland found in his researches, the character of the groove made by the diamond point had much to do with the brilliancy of the spectrum.

Dr. Alfred M. Mayer was another visitor who came to see us, whose memory has always been very dear to me. He was, at the time of his visit, the Professor of Physics at Stevens Institute, Hoboken, New Jersey. He brought his son Alfred with him, who later became a noted student of science and the head of the Department of Marine Biology of the Carnegie Research Institution at Washington.

Professor Mayer had written a series of articles in the "Scientific American Supplement," a paper just in its first years of issue, on the "Refinements of Modern Measurements," which I had read with the deepest interest; and as he had heard of our efforts in that line, he came all the way from his home in Orange, New Jersey, to spend a day with us. And a day of delightful reminiscences it was to us!

When he left our home on the hill, I went with him to the street-car, and then concluded to enjoy his company to the last. So I went over to the Union Station with him. The street-car was warm from the heat of a stove and there was no ventilation. When the conductor came in for the fares, Professor Mayer asked him to open some of the ventilators at the top of the car, but the conductor paid no attention to him. Just as he closed the door after collecting our fares, Professor Mayer got up and punched

out one of the glass windows in the ventilators. As the
conductor did not see him do it, it was blamed on some
one throwing a stone from the street. I confess I was a
little frightened by Professor Mayer's belligerency, but it
served that conductor right; I am sure my readers will
say ·"Amen."

Later on I was a guest at his home in New Jersey. He
had invented a heliostat which condensed the sun's rays
so they might be used, when passed through a microscope,
to throw magnified images upon a screen. He wanted us
to make one of these instruments for him, so I went to
his home to talk it over. I can well remember how he
took me out to the lawn to show me his skill in casting a
fly in trout fishing. He stood me up as the son of "Tell"
and cast that fly all around and very close to me. I confess I did not feel very comfortable while he was going
through his manipulations.

Of course my increasing acquaintanceship with scientific men led to more orders and still more. In 1885 I had
five assistants, and the press of work was so great that I
was faced with the problem of either moving to a larger
workshop or enlarging the one I was in. I have mentioned
before the fact that the Good Samaritan William Thaw had
taken an interest in my work and helped me over many
financial difficulties. For in spite of the increasing size
and scope of my work, I never seemed to be able to make
money. That part of the business did not interest me very
much and, besides, I was continually having to put money
back into the business for new machines, tools, etc. So
Mr. Thaw had been very generous with me. This, he carefully explained, was all done in the interest of science. He

wrote me once, regarding a salary of six hundred dollars a
year he was paying me in quarterly installments:

While I think highly of you and your wife and take pleasure
in opening the way for your work, nevertheless my appropria-
tions to your enterprises are primarily contributions to original
research in science, it being my privilege to judge for myself in
the matter and to regard you and your work as being as eminently entitled to support as if you were a chartered institution
and bore a sounding title. It is not a personal question in my
estimation, but a public interest I am serving in keeping you at
your special work.

I am reminded, too, that he was not altogether in sympathy with my business methods, or rather my lack of
them. In another letter I had from him in 1885 he wrote:

I must insist on your requiring payment before delivery
hereafter, for everything you sell, except in cases where the pay
is absolutely sure at a near and specified time, or in cases when
it may be wise to send an instrument for other than money-
earning purposes. As to —— and —— they discover instinc-
tively that you are a devotee to your specialty and without any
commercial greed or experience and they simply trifle with you.
You can afford hereafter to let them go unless they pay down,
and unless you adopt rigid business rules and methods in this
part of your work, you will be worn out with petty annoyances
and losses.

And again during that same year:

You have to make up a method of computing the cost of your
products, including material, time of skilled work, proper charge
for use of plant; and having that, add ten per cent for your
supervision. If you will master that suggestion, you will soon
be able to know what prices you should put on your product.
At present you do not know except that you know you don't
get enough out of your products to pay for them and leave you a
living.

But in addition to Mr. Thaw's business acumen, he had

a true appreciation of science, and was sympathetic with my struggles for perfection in every piece of work I undertook. He saw, with the increasing orders that were coming to me, that I must have enlarged quarters and suggested my moving across the river to the hill on which the Observatory stood. I had continued to work with Professor Langley, in whose investigations Mr. Thaw was keenly interested, and our work was so intimately blended that it seemed a wise move to have my shop nearer the Observatory. Mr. Thaw owned about half an acre of ground at the junction of Buena Vista Street and Perrysville Road, a couple of hundred yards from the Observatory. He proposed this as the site of new shops for me, and I was soon at work on plans for the shop, machinery, etc. I did not relish the work involved in moving from the top of one hill to the top of another about four miles distant, but there was amelioration in the fact that I was to be situated in one of the nicest, coziest, lightest, cleanest spots in the country.

I think Mr. Thaw's help at this particular time can best be explained by a letter I received from him then:

I am glad you are at work on your plan and machinery and that you have Mr. Rodd to help you in matters you are not familiar with. I leave the shops, size, and location of the buildings and underground entirely to your choice. The probable cost when the plans are settled on is a matter we will then confer upon. I think you will be scared when you see the estimate Mr. Rodd will make of the cost. They should be firm solid buildings. The material, I presume, will include wood, iron, brick, and stone, the general framing and roof, of wood. The machines you mention are not extravagant.

As I furnish the ground, the cost of buildings, and the cost of all new machinery, I think the better way to define the use and tenure of the place would be to give you a lease free of rent for ground, buildings, and the new machinery for five years, and the privilege to put in the machinery you have, and take it out again — the lease terminable by your death or disability, and its extension beyond five years to be left to me or my heirs. This would leave the use of the place and machinery your business, and give you a field in which to develop your capacity to make the works self-sustaining in producing instruments of precision and scientific appliances — you conducting the work, and its commercial or business aspects, while I furnish the ground, the buildings, and all new machinery free of charge and subject to your use.

We began to excavate in early March, 1886, and in May I was all moved. I had a machine shop twenty by forty-two feet, with beautiful light and surroundings. I put in a splendid forty-four-inch swing lathe made expressly for me, a fifteen by seventeen shaper, and a fine ten-horse-power engine. My motive energy was natural gas, of whose virtues I have previously spoken. Over the machine shop were the pattern shop and stock patterns — a nice band saw and lathe. In the boiler and engine room I placed my rough grinders to save dirt from the fine work. In the optical shop there were two heavy benches for machines, a bench and sink for silvering, one for making' polishers, and nicely arranged cupboards and shelves. I had my drawing table in the office, where I kept my finished work.

The testing cellar, according to Professor Langley, was perhaps the most complete in this country. There was an eighteen-inch air space all around it and a cement floor. In the dividing-engine room were six windows; and the earth outside the stone wall was low enough for splendid light, the windows being double. It could be heated automatically, and kept at a regular temperature. A door was provided in the partition so that, in case I had any long glasses to test, this door could be thrown open. Two heavy posts were cemented down deep into the floor, and did not touch the building at any place. They ran up into the optical room, where the glass was placed on its support, and then slid down into the cellar by rope-pulleys, counterpoise — all attached to the uprights. I had never dreamed of having anything so nice. And one of the best features was that I had a magnificent view for twelve miles down the Ohio and over every point of the compass save the east. All this Mr. Thaw did for me, not, he said, for charity, but to help push outward the boundary line of human knowledge. How I prayed for the ability to give a good account of my stewardship!

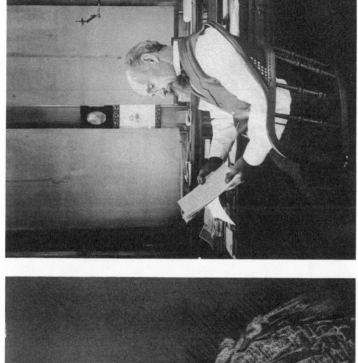

Phoebe Brashear. Portrait by E. M. Silverberg, 1911.
Brashear Association

John Brashear in his office.
Brashear Association

John Brashear with a group of children, 1916.
Brashear Association

William Thaw. Portrait by Charles Walz.
University of Pittsburgh Art Gallery

Samuel P. Langley.
University of Pittsburgh Archives

The Brashears' South Side house, 3 Holt Street.
Brashear Association

John Brashear's workshops, new and old.
Brashear Association

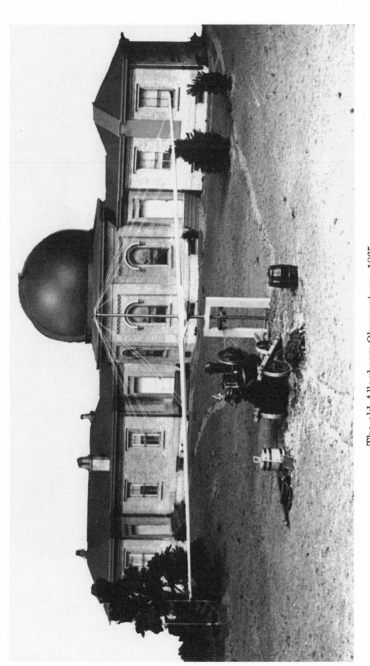

The old Allegheny Observatory, 1865.
University of Pittsburgh Archives

Entrance to the new Allegheny Observatory.
University of Pittsburgh Archives

CHAPTER XII

FIRST TRIP TO EUROPE

My first journey to Europe (1888) was made possible through the kindness of Henry Phipps, who desired me to chaperon his son. I talked it over with Mr. Thaw, and we decided it would be wise for me to accept Mr. Phipps's invitation, and that I should take my wife with me. He very generously insisted on giving me extra money for our journey, insisting that I should waste no time in walking to places I could go to by conveyance. This proved a very wise suggestion; for when one goes abroad, time is an element which must be taken into consideration.

I took with me letters of introduction to eminent scientists in Europe; to quite a number of whom we had furnished apparatus, especially the Rowland Diffraction Gratings. We secured passage on the steamer Chicago, where we had very comfortable quarters assigned to us, but, alas, alas, we had not sailed very far from port when our stomachs began to rebel, and my wife was forced to spend several days in bed. I tried to fight it out, but I do not remember ever spending three more miserable days than on this my first voyage. However, there is usually one consolation in seasickness. After two or three days you begin to get over it and become so independent of the threats of old Neptune that you pay no more attention to him than if you were on a quiet river steamer.

We arrived at Liverpool, where we had to go through the usual formality of the customs examination. I learned a lesson from that first examination, too. I had taken over a beautiful six-inch diffraction grating for Dr. Hasselberg, of Stockholm, which I wanted to show to Sir James Dewar, his associate, Professor Liveing, and other physicists whom I should likely meet on my travels. I carried the box containing the grating in my hands, and the customs officer made me show it to him. It was all I could do to prevent him from rubbing his hands over the beautiful surface and the ruled lines! I told him I had brought it with me to show to the scientific men I should meet, and finally induced him to pass it without appraisement or detention, although his curiosity was greatly excited by the beauty of the colors that he saw on its surface. I did not feel like running the risk of showing the grating to another customs officer, so I provided myself with a fine chamois skin, and thereafter, when I had to pass through customs houses, I would take the grating out of its case, wrap it in the chamois, and put it in my overcoat pocket. It weighed at least ten pounds, and I am sure my overcoat on that side was two inches longer than on the other before I got through with my journey.

At that time a six-inch diffraction grating was a marvel of scientific precision, of a size hitherto undreamed of; and I knew of nothing that would create more interest among the scientific men to whom I should have the pleasure of showing it, than that splendid piece of work by Professor Rowland.

We did not delay in Liverpool very long; but one incident comes to my mind very forcibly which occurred while we were there. I have always been very fond of youngsters, no matter what country I have met them in, and one of my first impulses is to do something to make friends with them. Seeing a lot of ragged urchins gathered around Nelson's Monument, I bought two or three pounds of candy and walked down among the boys — about as tough-looking a set as I ever have seen, some of them half-naked. It was some time before I could get any of them to come near me, but I was going to bribe them with some candy if they would tell me their names. Alas for me! When they found I had candy in my possession, I was nearly mobbed. Had I not been able to toss the bag away from me, I believe they would have torn my clothes from me. That scramble I shall never forget, although I confess I did not turn to look at them until I got far enough away to retreat in good order if they got after me.

One of the things that distressed me very much both in Liverpool and in London was to observe through the windows and open doors of the liquor saloons that most of the bartenders were women. To me it was a sad comment on woman's position; and I learned that the practice existed not only in London and Liverpool, but in many other towns in England.

While in London we visited the works of our friend Adam Hilger and also the works of John Browning, at that time two of the most celebrated optical-instrument makers in the city. We also visited the Greenwich Observatory, where we were received with great kindness by the staff, and were shown through by our friend Mr. Maunder.

I met no more delightful person in London than Mr. Maw, who with Mr. Dredge edited and published "Engineering," perhaps the greatest engineering publication in the world. Mr. Maw had published a splendid illustrated account of the Lick Observatory and the Princeton Spectrograph, and was the treasurer of the Royal Astronomical Society, of which I had the honor to be made a member in 1892. We spent a delightful evening as the guests of Mr. and Mrs. Maw at their home in Kensington, where he had a six-inch telescope and an observatory which I enjoyed studying very much.

Here I wish to pay a tribute to Sir James Dewar (then Dr. Dewar), who was then in charge of the Royal Institution. He not only gave me the freedom of the Institution, but secured for me cards for the Zoölogical Gardens, and was most kind in every way. My wife and I were the guests of Sir James and Lady Dewar at a delightful luncheon, and I can well remember Sir James asking Mrs. Brashear "if she would have a slice of good *English* roast beef from *Chicago*."

On one of my visits to the Royal Institution I was shown many things of great historic interest, among them Sir Humphry Davy's first safety lamp, which was nothing more than a flat spiral coil of wire with a stem of the same wire extending down to a base; but it effectively stopped the flame of a lamp from extending through the interstices of the flat spiral.

Another was one of the earliest, if not the first, balance used by Cavendish in his chemical experiments and investigations. But the most interesting of all was the original dynamo made by Michael Faraday which, with other precious instruments invented and used by pioneers in science, was kept in a case with double doors, which I have always liked to name "the holy of holies."

When Dr. Dewar placed the little machine in my hands (it did not weigh over ten pounds as I remember), he asked me if I knew what it was. Replying in the negative, he told me it was the original dynamo made by Faraday, "the father and mother of all the wonderful electric energy of to-day." Remember, my reader, this was in 1888. What has come to us since in the evolution of Faraday's invention!

I also had the pleasure of visiting the celebrated works of R. & J. Beck, at that time the most noted microscope and photographic lens makers in London; and, of course, we spent many pleasant hours in the British Museum.

While in London we received an invitation from Mr. and Mrs. Carnegie to visit them at their home at Sunningdale. Here we received a royal welcome. They had as their guests at that time Mr. Abbott, of Pittsburgh, one of the partners of the Carnegie Steel Company, and his wife, and a Scotch sculptor who had been making a bust of Mr. Carnegie, and who was about to return to his home in Scotland at the same time we were leaving. Mr. Carnegie proposed that he send us all to Slough in his own conveyance, where we wanted to visit the home of the Herschels. It was a wonderful ride that we had in that open coach, with coachman and footman. We passed along the parks surrounding Windsor Castle before we reached the home of the Herschels, the home celebrated in astronomical annals for the great work done there by Sir William and Sir John Herschel.

When we reached the town, the coachman stopped while I asked several gentlemen standing at a street corner where the home of the Herschels was. Not one of them knew; but when I told them he was a great astronomer and had an observatory in the town, one of them remarked that there was a house not two blocks away called "Observatory House." I walked to the spot while the coachman drove slowly along the way. The little home was covered with vines, but the name "Observatory House" had been kept clear of them. I knocked on the door with the old-fashioned knocker; and when the door was opened to me, the first thing I saw in the hallway was one of the famous "seven-foot" reflecting telescopes made by the hands of Herschel and his workman. He rarely ever gave the diameter of his telescopes, but called them "seven-foot," "ten-foot," etc.

My wife and I accepted the invitation to "Come in." Entering the hall, the next thing that caught my eye was the forty-eight-inch reflecting speculum mirror that was hung in a niche in the wall, the bolt that held it passing up through the ceiling to the floor above. This famous old mirror was worked by the hands of Sir William Herschel himself. The story goes that he was occasionally fed by his sister as he walked around the mirror, putting the final correcting strokes upon it. It retained a fair polish, at least until I saw it last. It was of deep interest to me as I looked at it and thought over the work that had been accomplished with it by Sir William and his devoted sister Caroline.

We were not long in getting acquainted with the four daughters of Sir John Herschel and his son Alexander.

Tea was prepared for us, as is the usual custom in England, and Alexander Herschel came and sat with us. We were afterward told that it was a rare thing for him to sit down at the table with others of the family.

After a delightful chat in the home, we were taken out into the yard where there still remained the circle, like a circus ring, in the center of which the great telescope was originally mounted. It was on New Year's Eve, 1839–40, that the telescope was taken down, the great tube laid at the side of the garden, and the family gathered in the tube and sang the requiem of "The Old Telescope":

> In the old Telescope's tube we sit,
> And the shades of the past around us flit;
> His requiem sing we with shout and din,
> While the old year goes out and the new comes in.
>
> Full fifty years did he laugh at the storm,
> And the blast could not shake his majestic form;
> Now prone he lies, where he once stood high,
> And searched the deep heaven with his broad, bright eye.

At the time of our visit the old tube had all been destroyed or carried away except about eight feet of the end in which the speculum rested. A tree had fallen upon the tube and mashed it in badly, and parts of it had been carried away by relic-hunters. But the two cast-iron wheels and axle that supported them at the lower end of the telescope were still intact, although badly rusted.

I find the following note in my own hand, on the margin of Newcomb's "Popular Astronomy," beside the description of the old telescope:

When Mrs. B. and I visited Slough in 1888 the old tube had all been destroyed or carried away but about eight feet of the end in which the speculum rested. I sat on this old relic, and Ma always insists that I hugged and kissed it.   J. A. B.

When I saw the large mirror, it did not have a polish for the finer work; but I was astonished to find it as good as it was.

After we saw the old tube of the Herschel telescope, we were taken up into the second story of the old brick building where Caroline Herschel did most of her computations in the reduction of her brother's observations. There was a barrel of old manuscripts sitting in the room, which had been discarded by her, and if ever I was tempted to steal anything as a relic, it was to take some of the manuscripts out of that barrel. In perusing the memoirs of Caroline Herschel I have often thought of that visit; and when I have considered the days and nights she worked with her brother, sometimes having but a few hours' sleep through the week, I have felt keenly her injustice to herself in her remark concerning the work she had done for her brother, that "an educated puppy dog would have done as well."

On our return to the house, Alexander Herschel took me into his study where he showed me some interesting studies he had made of the rhythmic lines in the spectrum. He had drawn these lines with colored crayons, and I had the great pleasure to bring some copies home with me. This was pioneer work in the study of rhythmic lines that was later on beautifully corroborated by the photographs of the spectrum. It was with great reluctance we left the home of the Herschels.

During this same visit to Europe, while I was the guest of Dr. Dewar, of the Royal Institution, and of Dr. Liveing, I was invited to visit Cambridge, where I had the great privilege of examining one of the five-and-one-half-inch reflecting telescopes made by Sir Isaac Newton. I was allowed to take the speculum out of the telescope and examine it. After an interval of perhaps one hundred and fifty years the surface was still fairly bright, and would no doubt show bright stars or planets quite well.

I must not forget a pleasant occurrence at the time of this visit to Cambridge. During the visit of the British Association to Montreal and Philadelphia in 1884, I had become acquainted with John Adams, the co-discoverer with Leverrier of the planet Neptune. On the occasion of my visit to Cambridge, as I was walking from the depot toward Saint John's College, I had the good fortune to meet Professor Adams and his wife. He was far from well at the time, and was out for a walk for his health. I stopped to have a chat with the great man who, had the value of his computation been recognized, would have been the first discoverer of Neptune.

We said good-bye to England and had a pleasant ride to Paris. My first visit was to the Paris Observatory, where I met Paul and Prosper Henry, the two celebrated French astronomers who had already done some splendid work in astronomical photography. Indeed, while Rutherfurd in America and others in England had already done much in this field of work, it was for the Henry brothers to begin a systematic study of a zone of the heavens which had been assigned to the Paris Observatory for a careful study of the position of the stars. When their work reached the neighborhood of the Milky Way, they found that a visual telescopic study of the stars in the zone down to the magnitude decided upon by the Astronomical Photographic Congress would take a lifetime. So they constructed a photographic telescope which recorded stars on plates that, after development, could be studied in the laboratory by assistants whose time was not so valuable as that of the observers. This was soon adopted as the ideal way to make a survey of the principal stars of the heavens. Indeed, as I write these lines the finest telescopes in the world are devoted entirely to photographic studies of the heavens, and the visual telescope has had its best days. Not only has the telescope been applied to photographing the heavens, but stellar-spectrum photography has opened a new field of research, and has told us more than all else of the constitution of the universe of stars, their motion in the line of sight, and the approximate distance of the binary systems.

Not only were the Henry brothers great astronomers, but they had constructed the optical parts of their own telescopes, and had made some of the largest and best telescopes for the French observatories. When I visited their workshop, they very unselfishly showed me their work and how they did it; and even went so far as to insist on instructing me in methods of paper-polishing which they used exclusively, and also their methods of testing optical surfaces.

Once they insisted upon our staying with them for dinner. They lived very modestly, but had they lived in a palace we should not have enjoyed it more. Those dear fellows had great big hearts and a human side which was so delightfully shown to us that we felt almost as if we were in our own home. I can remember how they went down into their cellars and got the richest old wines that had been saved for many years to offer them to us; and although we were not wine-drinkers, we certainly had to taste the delicious beverages they placed before us. After the dinner was over, we discovered that they were in possession of a Mason & Hamlin melodeon. My wife and I sat down and sang some of our favorite songs for them, and the applause we got will never be forgotten. When we sang one of Stephen Foster's melodies, they both shouted "Bis, bis, encore!" We stayed so late that night that, their home being in the suburbs, they had to accompany us in a cab in order to get us to the city. For years after our visit with them, their letters would remind us of "the charming musicale" we gave them at their home.

During our stay in Paris I visited the celebrated works of Gautier, who constructed the instrumental parts of the French telescopes as well as those of other countries. I also visited the works of Bardou, a firm that made many small telescopes and field-glasses. Here I ordered a number of objectives for finders for telescopes and spectroscopes, and paid an extra price for them; but when we received them at home, we found them so badly corrected that they could not be used. I never have been able to understand this failure on the part of M. Bardou, as he had a very excellent reputation for high-class work.

Our visit to the Observatory of Meudon was one of the greatest interest to me. If I remember correctly, Dr. Janssen, the director, was at that time president of the Academy of Sciences in France. We had furnished him with a beautiful diffraction grating, and had had considerable correspondence with him. We were delighted with the reception he gave us. After an examination of the instruments in the Observatory, we took a walk through the spacious and beautiful grounds where was being erected a large refractor, the lenses for which were being made by the Henry brothers. Dr. Janssen took me to the wall that surrounded that part of the Observatory grounds, and showed me the spot where he started off in a balloon loaded with his observing outfit, and sailed over the German army to Algiers, for the purpose of observing the total eclipse of the sun. He alighted near the coast of France on a farm; and after the farmers got over the excitement of his landing, he was treated to one of the most delicious chicken dinners that he had tasted for months, as the people of Paris had been living on horse-flesh and almost any edible they could get hold of during the siege of Paris.

I became very fond of him. Astronomers will remember that he had an observatory built on the top of Mont Blanc; was carried there by Swiss guides, and made some valuable records of high-mountain observations.

I remember that he told me of gathering the snow from the Observatory reservation, piling it up about fifteen feet high, and placing certain instruments on top of it, as an experiment that would possibly give him information as to how the observatory should be built on the snowy and ice-capped Mont Blanc.

During this visit to Paris, I had in my hands the four-inch lens of single material — crown glass — and of twenty-five-feet focus, with which Domenico Cassini discovered the real character of Saturn's rings, which was problematical as seen in the little telescope of Galileo.

We left Paris with many pleasant memories of its scientific men and their families, who had made us so welcome.

Our next objective was Switzerland. The journey was a very delightful one, and we landed at Lausanne late at night. We passed through some beautiful and interesting country but did not stop on our way, as we did on our trip four years later. We were glad to go to rest in our delightful room in the hotel at Lausanne. I wakened at the dawn of day, and from my window there lay before me the beautiful Lake of Geneva. Across on the other side I saw what I thought were light clouds hovering far over the horizon, but as the sun came up I saw they were snow-capped mountains in all their beauty, and the grandeur of this my first view of the Swiss mountains enthralled me. My expressions of wonder wakened my wife, and together we sat there, watching the sun come up from the horizon and illuminate the snow-capped peaks.

We did not stay at Lausanne very long. We went by steamer to Geneva where we stayed overnight, and in the morning left for Chamonix, at which point guides were secured to take us on our various mountain trips. Our first ascent of the mountain was by La Flégère, where we first saw the wonderful glaciers of Switzerland. We crossed over one of them with our guides — a very dangerous walk — but we kept away from the crevasses, which were enormously deep, probably one eighth of a mile. The ladies rode up the mountain on mules, but as I never had a liking for that kind of travel, my friend Mr. Beevers and I walked with the guides.

Leaving Chamonix after a delightful stay of several days, we took conveyance to Brieg, and after a short sojourn there, we started for the Lake of Constance, passing over the Furka Pass, the highest point we had reached in Switzerland.

Reaching our port on Lake Constance, we took a boat and went across to the borders of Germany. Here we took a train, and after a ride in a hot compartment, we reached Munich late in the evening. Our train stopped at a halfway place, and as there was no drinking water to be had, I rushed out into the station and found long tables covered with beer mugs, filled to the brim, and ready for passengers to grab. I paid for two, rushed off to the train, handing one of them to my wife through the window of the car, and swallowing the other myself. Germany has a reputation for her beer, particularly in Munich. As I always disliked the taste of anything of a bitter nature, it was like taking a dose of nasty medicine to swallow the mug of beer, but it was a "Hobson's choice."

When we arrived in Munich, we found it impossible to get quarters at the hotel to which we had been directed. We found comfortable quarters in a *pension* and were as kindly received as if we had been members of the family. Indeed, the two maids of the house took such a liking to us that they wanted to come to America with us.

There was an exposition held in Munich at the time of our visit which enabled us to see many of the products of Germany that we could not have seen otherwise. Among the places of deep interest to us was the workshop of Fraunhofer, who constructed the first telescope lenses by scientific methods.

From Munich we took train to Leipsic where we found excellent quarters in the Hotel Hauffe. We were scarcely settled when we heard a great shouting outside the hotel. I ran to the end of the hall, and as I went down the stairway a blackboard in the office attracted my attention. I found the name of General von Moltke at the head of the list of hotel guests, and our names at the end of it, as we were the last to come in. We at once went down and joined the crowd. Von Moltke came out on the balcony in front of his room at the corner of the building and made a brief address to the people; then some one started to sing "The Watch on the Rhine," in which Ma and I both joined. Von Moltke retired, the crowd dispersed, and we went back to our room for a much-needed rest.

Our first visit in Leipsic was to Dr. Schumann, who, even at that time, was noted for researches in the ultraviolet region of the spectrum. We had furnished him with a beautiful grating, and the good fellow made us welcome at once, later on giving us a dinner at one of the fine restaurants in the city.

At that time he had photographed to wave-length about 1850, and showed us many photographs of his beautiful spectra.

From Leipsic we went to Berlin, my objective point being the great Potsdam Observatory for which we had furnished some apparatus, especially a fine grating for Dr. Scheiner. After a night's rest we secured a guide and started for Potsdam. On our way we met the German Emperor who had recently taken the throne. The guide called our attention to the Emperor coming toward us in a fine equipage, with three soldiers accompanying him. The Emperor was in undress uniform, but the others were gorgeously attired in their army suits, so we bowed most profoundly to one of these, thinking he was the Emperor. After he had passed, our guide informed us we had bowed to the wrong man.

We were received with great kindness at the Potsdam Observatory, although the director was absent. Dr. Scheiner had done some wonderful work in spectrum analysis, and had written a book on astrophysics which was later translated by Dr. Frost, of the Yerkes Observatory.

From Berlin we went to Hamburg where I visited the famous works of the Repsold brothers. They were at the time constructing a heliometer for Dr. Gill, of the Cape of Good Hope. I was also shown the dividing-engine which, at the time, was the best in the world. I was treated with royal courtesy by the two brothers, and every facility given me to study their methods. One thing which impressed me was that all their drawings were made full-size and with great accuracy; but, as I remember, no figures were placed upon them, all dimensions being taken by measurements of the drawings. I presume that no precision work was ever done with greater accuracy at the time of my visit than was done by the Repsold brothers.

Hamburg was a beautiful place to visit, and many a pleasant ride Ma and I took on the lake in front of the city; and as our hotel was very near the border of the water, we would frequently go for an hour's ride in a rowboat. We made a short journey to Antwerp, visiting the wonderful zoölogical gardens, and the art gallery which contains so many of the pictures of Rubens.

It was our intention to go from Hamburg to Stockholm,

but our time was becoming limited, as we had overstayed in Munich. We had also given up our intended trip to Italy. So we took a vessel for Queensboro. This was a night journey and we did not sleep very comfortably, as the rolling of the sea and the snoring of our next-door neighbor kept us awake most of the time. From this point we went to London for a brief stay and took a train north to Edinburgh.

At Edinburgh we visited the old Observatory of Piazzi Smyth, but he had gone to Crova. After a pleasant stay in Edinburgh for a few days we left for Glasgow, where I hoped to meet Sir William Thomson at the university; but as it was vacation time, he had gone off for a yachting trip with Helmholtz. They were great friends and lovers of yachting. I had the pleasure, however, of meeting a number of professors at the University of Glasgow.

There was a large exposition being held at Glasgow which gave me an opportunity to study the products of Scotland. Here we saw some of the immense shafts which were made for the ships that were being built on the Clyde. Leaving Glasgow we went down the river Clyde, and then sailed for Belfast. Here for the first time I saw the magnificent phosphorescence of the ocean as we left the harbor. I have never seen anything quite so beautiful in the sea.

We arrived in Belfast on Sunday morning and actually had to bribe the jaunting-car driver to take us to the hotel. Some walked to their destination; but some of us managed to hire these unique conveyances, and we reached our hotel glad to have crossed the Channel without being seasick. We arrived in time to go to a Presby-

terian Church, as we were told there was quite a famous
minister to preach that day and that a Scotch-Irish regi-
ment was to attend the services. The choir was seated
away up near the ceiling at the end of the church, far
above the pulpit; but they sang well, and we were delighted to hear music sung by those whose language we
understood.

From Belfast we went to Dublin, our objective point
being the works of Sir Howard Grubb, the most famous
works, probably, in Great Britain, for the construction of
large telescopes. It was Sir Howard Grubb, Sr., who
made the great Melbourne reflecting telescope, and his
son made the refractor for the observatory at Vienna and
practically all the modern telescopes for the Greenwich
Observatory. We were given a warm welcome by Sir
Howard, but he was feeling very sad over the recent loss
of his only son and expressed his regret at not being able
to have us as his guests. However, every facility was
given me to study his works and methods of manipulation;
and as he, with his father, had been in business for many
years, some valuable lessons were to be learned from his
experiences.

Dublin University was not in session, but we met a
number of the professors. One especially, Professor
Adeney, was very kind to us. We had furnished him a
concave grating with which he had done some excellent
work.

Leaving Dublin we went to Cork. On account of sailing
so soon we were unable to visit the celebrated Lakes of
Killarney, much to our regret. At the junction of the
railroad to Killarney, a number of friends from Pittsburgh

who had had the good fortune to visit the Lakes were returning on their way to Cork and Queenstown, whence we were to embark by lighter for the steamer.

We had not long to stay in Cork, but we were besieged by Irish women to buy the things they had for sale, from donkeys to little pots of shamrock. We did not buy any donkeys, but we did bring some shamrock home with us. Our lighter took us out to the new steamer, the City of New York.

We had a beautiful view of Queenstown as we passed out of the harbor; but seemed to have no regret at leaving the shores of Ireland, as we were going to our native land. No greater joy could fill our hearts than that which we experienced as we came in sight of the harbor of New York, and landed on the shores of dear old America. We hurried on to Pittsburgh where we were given a rousing welcome by our dear ones and friends at our home on Observatory Hill.

CHAPTER XIII

TRIP TO GREAT BRITAIN

In the early spring of 1892 I had a telegram from Mr. Carnegie asking me to come on to New York to help out with a scientific exhibit that he had brought home from the Gesellschaft Urania in Berlin. The exhibit, with its lectures on astronomy, geology, and kindred sciences, had become so popular in Berlin that it is said ninety thousand men, women, and children attended in one year. The exhibition and lectures had been running for some time at Carnegie Music Hall in New York, but had been a failure, mostly because the lectures which accompanied the various scenes as they were either thrown on a screen or shown through mechanical or electrical devices, were read by an elocutionist instead of by some one who had a real knowledge of the subject and who could enter into the spirit of it.

My friend Keeler, of the Allegheny Observatory, and Mr. Reed, of the Camden (New Jersey) Observatory, went with me to hear one of the lectures delivered by the elocutionist. The poor fellow did the best he could, but it was like the play of "Hamlet" with Hamlet left out. The lectures were postponed for two or three days, and it was proposed to reopen on the following Monday. Mr. Carnegie had sent for me because he was very desirous that I should undertake the astronomical lectures, which

I agreed to do. I had worked almost up to the elastic limit before starting for New York, but I at once undertook to correlate the astronomical exhibit with the lecture that was to be given. I worked steadily in my room at the hotel until long after midnight; indeed, until I fell asleep in my chair. Awakening an hour afterward, I went to bed, and in a few minutes found that something was the matter with me, as the room was whirling around like a top and my heart going at about one hundred and sixty per minute. The hotel physician was called and pronounced it overwork. Mr. Carnegie's physician, Dr. Garmany, was called early in the morning, and pronounced my trouble a physical breakdown, or, in common parlance, nervous prostration. I was immediately sent home, passing a sleepless night on the train, was put to bed, and stayed there for six weeks before I began to make any improvement. As soon as I was able to be out at all, I was sent for by Mr. Carnegie, who had come to Pittsburgh, and a trip to Europe was at once suggested. I was afraid to undertake the journey; but he insisted that nothing would be better medicine for me than a trip across the ocean, and I finally consented.

Henry Phipps had sent us an invitation to come to Knebworth Castle, the former home of Lord Lytton's family. We went there first and spent a delightful week on one of the most beautiful estates in England. The great entrance hall of the castle was full of armor and other relics of the past; and the upper hallway was decorated from one end to the other with original sketches made to illustrate Bulwer's novels. Some of the bedrooms were fitted up with old historic furniture, and some of the bedsteads would weigh, I should say, almost a ton. The windows in our room faced the sunrise; and as the brilliant red curtains had been pulled down by the maid when we retired, the glare of the morning sun was shining through them when we awoke. Our first impression was that the castle was on fire, and I assure you I was not long in getting out of bed. I was pleasantly undeceived, however, as I pushed up the curtain. From our window we could see a row of trees that grew so closely together that nothing could be seen beyond them. We afterward learned that Lady Lytton had become displeased with the minister of the little church that was on the estate and, not being able to depose him, she had the trees set out so that no view of the church could be had from the castle.

We attended church on the Sabbath we stayed there, and found a sort of a box arrangement had been made so that the family could enter, close the gate, and shut themselves off from the balance of the congregation. We sat there with the family while all the workmen and employees and their wives and families occupied the seats below us. As I remember, the music was very good; but to me the service did not seem to have the human side to it, for the entire congregation had just as much right to hear the Gospel from a box as we had.

Our host and hostess were very kind to us and planned delightful rides around the country. As it was springtime, the foliage and early flowers were very beautiful indeed. We enjoyed these trips to the utmost; my health seemed to take on new vigor, and I began to feel like myself again. Leaving Knebworth, we went to London, where we found quarters in the *pension* where we had stopped before.

While in London I, of course, visited the Royal Institution where our friends Sir James and Lady Dewar always gave us a welcome. Mr. Maw, the editor of "Engineering," invited us to his home in South Kensington to meet his family, dine with them, and enjoy a study of his unique observatory in which he had a six-inch Cooke Equatorial Telescope. I was also invited to the annual dinner of the Royal Astronomical Society.

I had attended one of their meetings, where I was requested to tell the Society something of the status of astronomy in America. I met a number of eminent astronomers at that meeting, among them the son of Lord Rosse, of Parsonstown, Ireland, whose father had constructed a seventy-two-inch reflecting telescope which was erected on the estate near Parsonstown. The younger Lord Rosse gave me a cordial invitation to bring my wife and spend a week with them. I should have liked to accept the invitation, as I had read so much about the great telescope, but it would have broken into our time very considerably, and I had learned that, although we should be the guests of Lord Rosse, the fees expected by the servants at our departure would deplete our pocketbooks to such an extent we might have nothing left to finish our travels!

The annual dinner of the Royal Astronomical Society was one of the most delightful episodes of our visit to London. There was only one other American invited, no less a personage than George W. Hill, the great mathematician. Cambridge University had voted an honorary degree for him, and he was in England to receive it. Christie, the Astronomer Royal, was there, as were Dr. Common, Mr. Maw, Dr. Knobel, Mr. Maunder, and others. It was certainly a royal event for me, for I was received with the greatest kindness, and I could not help but have an occasional thought that it was only a few years since I was a greasy millwright in Pittsburgh. There is one thing that can be said of science and scientific men and women. While social lines, particularly in England, are drawn very close, science has no boundaries of this kind. This fact I noticed particularly in an evening with the British Association. This Society had in its member-ship many amateurs who loved astronomy, but who worked at regular vocations, some of which were of menial character, but if they had done good work in adding to the sum of knowledge in the beautiful science of astronomy, they were honored and received as kindly as if they were the greatest moguls of the country. I think that scientific men respect the work of enthusiastic amateurs, if that work is done in a conscientious, careful manner.

Among the interesting persons I met at the British Association was Miss Agnes Clerke, whose works on the history of astronomy are second to none. We paid a visit to the home of Sir William Huggins and his wife, to whom he has given so much credit for her part in his astronomical research. While we were there on one of our visits to in-spect the Observatory, we were invited to take a cup of tea with them. While we were at tea, Dr. Knobel, Secre-tary of the Royal Astronomical Society, dropped in and of course was invited to join us. Dr. Huggins said to me,

"Mr. Brashear, you will imagine Dr. Knobel has come to talk astronomy, but in this you are mistaken, for he has come to talk violin." I soon learned that Dr. Huggins was a violinist of no mean ability; and his wife presided at the pipe organ which was in the room where we took tea.

Music and astronomy have always gone well together. Sir William Herschel was a noted organist of his day. All his brothers were musicians; and Caroline remarked, upon coming home from a concert she had attended at Hanover, that she had been to hear Ole Bull play the violin, but his playing could not touch the music of her brother Dietrich.

We had furnished Dr. Huggins with the optical equipment for one of his star spectroscopes. We had already constructed several star spectroscopes, and had sent blueprints of one of them to Dr. Huggins, advising him to have the spectroscope built in Europe under his own supervision, and telling him that he was at liberty to use any or all of the design as shown in the blueprint sent him. He frequently remarked that he had never known any business firm to send out their own designs for the free use of some one else. At his request I visited the Troughton & Simms Works, some distance outside of London, carrying with me a letter of introduction from him. They were at this time constructing a spectroscope for him, and although the firm seemed to be a little suspicious of me at first and did not treat me as they should have done a messenger from Dr. Huggins, yet I noticed several places where I could help them out of difficulties in the construction of the instrument, particularly that of the slit.

I finally won them over, and they seemed to appreciate what I told them so much that young Mr. Simms invited me to lunch with him. When I was introduced to him in the office he had made the remark that he supposed I had "come over to pick up methods that would be of use to us in our works at home." I declined the invitation to lunch, and went back to London with no great affection for the new representatives of this old and honored firm.

When I visited Cooke & Sons' Works, I received courteous treatment, as I did also at R. & J. Beck's; and, while I learned a few things that were of value to me, I tried to leave with them more than value received.

I may have mentioned in the earlier part of my story that I had appealed to Dr. John Tyndall, at that time the head of the Royal Institution of Great Britain, to help me solve some of the problems I had met with in my studies of light. This was while I was working in the rolling mill, away back in 1863. I thought it a pretty bold venture on my part, but I received a reply from Dr. Tyndall's secretary that gave me the information sought in plain, beautiful, and easily understood language. How proud I was of his interest! Twenty-nine years later I was going to make my second visit to Europe, and I wanted to take some kind of a present to the man who had lent me a helping hand nearly three decades before. I could think of nothing more likely to please a man of science than one of the Rowland Diffraction Gratings. I concluded to take one of these gratings with me to present to Professor Tyndall, together with two very accurate optical-glass bars that had been made as duplicates for an instrument

devised by my young friend Dr. George E. Hale. These
three pieces of accurate optical work I placed in a velvet-
lined case; and when I made my first visit to the Royal
Institution, I took the present with me to ask Dr. Dewar's
advice as to how I should get it to Professor Tyndall.

To my sorrow I learned that Professor Tyndall was very
ill, but Dr. Dewar suggested that I write to him, and he
would send the presents and my letter by messenger to
his home, remarking that Tyndall would appreciate the
gift and it would do him good. I followed his suggestions,
and in a day or two a letter came to me from the dear man
who had helped me so many years before. That letter
I had framed, and it has hung in my home for many years.
I would not part with it for gold or jewels.

With the letter came a copy of his last book, "New
Fragments," with the following inscription, written by
his amanuensis, but signed by his own hand on the fly-
leaf:

To his friend J. A. Brashear, to whom he wishes length of
days, and the reward of a genuine worker, this book is inscribed
by its author,

1892   JOHN TYNDALL

The book has been precious reading to me, not alone
for the scientific value, but for that masterly essay on the
Sabbath which in my humble opinion places Professor
Tyndall on the highest pedestal as an advocate of the
religion of humanity. Although there is still a lingering
of the doctrine that the Sabbath was not made for man,
I am rejoiced to know that music, flowers, the woods, the
fields, art — all things good and beautiful, things that
are ennobling and elevating to the human soul — are

open to all, even on the Sabbath day. How much of this God-given freedom we owe to this great man of science we shall never know; but I commend to the readers of this humble volume the first chapter of "New Fragments," and even if he read no farther he will know what a human man John Tyndall was.

What a name he has left behind him by the good he has done in bringing the abstruse things of our beloved science down to the comprehension of the layman, without sacrificing its truth for the mere sake of embellishment! Read his charming book on "Forms of Water in Snow and Ice." You will need no better evidence of the truth of what I have said of him. It has been one of the greatest delights of my life, now that I am able to look back upon seventy-nine years of it, that, starting and still occupying only a little niche in the workshop of this old world, so many men and women of the type of the successor of that master, Michael Faraday — John Tyndall — have been my friends.

During my visit in London I ran up to Cambridge, and paid a visit to Dr. Liveing, and by his invitation lunched with the faculty of one of the colleges. A dark liquid was served instead of the water at our American lunch-tables. One sip of it made me shake with its bitter taste. It was my only sip. I learned later on it was "brown stout," a very familiar beverage with the English, though I did not know it at the time. Later I was the guest of Professor Newall, whose father was one of the manufacturers of the first Atlantic cable. I brought a piece or specimen of the cable home with me which I later had the pleasure of presenting to my friend, Dean Wurtz, of the Department of

Electrical Engineering of the Carnegie Technical School, only a year or so ago.

I must not forget to record a visit I made to Piazzi Smyth, the English astronomer, who had moved from the old Observatory in Edinburgh where he was Astronomer Royal for Scotland, to Crova, a pretty town in England. At the time of my visit, he had in his home a fine private laboratory for physical research and was doing some interesting work in the domain of spectrum analysis. We had furnished him with a Rowland Diffraction Grating, which he was using with splendid results. I was greatly surprised to learn that he had one of the largest and most complete storage batteries I had ever seen. He told me that with the storage battery he could get a much steadier electric arc for his spectrum work than with the dynamos made at the time; and from the fine photographs he showed me of the spectra of several substances, I am sure he was right. It will be remembered that in his spectroscopic studies he called attention to the importance of the rainband absorption.

Perhaps he was best known by his book on "Our Inheritance in the Great Pyramid"; which, while considered by most students of science a paradox, contains an interesting account of his studies of this ancient structure. I can remember his words as we shook hands: "My dear Mr. Brashear, if you will stay all day with me, I will promise not to talk pyramid once while you are here." I told him I would stay until the last train to London whether he talked pyramid or not.

His wife was a great sufferer from rheumatism; but she was led to the lunch-table, and I had the honor to break bread not only with a great scientist, but with his wife whom he honored as all men should honor their companions in life's work. There is an adage that, "If a man becomes truly great, it is usually the help of a devoted wife that is responsible for it."

It was hard to leave our devoted friends in Europe, but then it was always good to get home and see the dear ones from whom we had been separated.

CHAPTER XIV

THE OLD ALLEGHENY OBSERVATORY AND PROFESSOR LANGLEY

FOR a period of thirty years following my first visit in 1876 to the old Allegheny Observatory I was associated with Professor Samuel P. Langley, a man of magnificent intellect, one never satisfied with a half-proved hypothesis, but always reaching out for final proof before he announced any of his great discoveries. He had been called to Pittsburgh in 1867 as Director of the old Allegheny Observatory and Professor of Astronomy at the Western University of Pennsylvania. The generosity of the man who was later to become my benefactor, William Thaw, soon released him from his teaching duties and gradually overcame the handicaps of the meager equipment of the Observatory in those early days, thus enabling Professor Langley to devote his entire time to the remarkable investigations which made the Allegheny Observatory famous among scientists throughout the world.

I confess that when I first knew Professor Langley I found him a cold, formal fellow, a man quite difficult to approach. I felt like a fish out of water in his presence, for I always want to feel free with every one I meet and have them feel the same with me. He used to lay out work he wanted me to do for him which I could reasonably

expect to give him, in the press of my other business, in a
month's time, but he must have it within two weeks and
was impatient with any delay. He was a bachelor, and
I remember an aunt of his once told him he needed a
first-class wife to keep him in trim.

But as I grew to know him better, I found he was neither
cold nor indifferent. I suppose few men ever came to know
him as I did. Many times I have walked miles with him
when nothing but monosyllables ever escaped his lips.
This was not because he was callous to my questions, but
because, when some intricate problem in solar physics
took possession of his mind, it excluded everything else.
At other times during our walks from the old Observatory
to the woods where the new Observatory now stands, his
conversation from the beginning to the end of our stroll
was entertaining and instructive.

In his studies in the domain of solar physics, Professor
Langley was early impressed with the idea that much of
the radiant energy from the sun was not recognized by
the instruments then in use, and after a long series of
experiments he discovered and developed that marvelously
delicate instrument, the bolometer. With that instrument he began a series of investigations upon the sun, the
moon, and the stars which brought to light some of the most
important factors in the whole range of astronomical physics. During these years he would constantly send for me
to carry out certain of the mechanical details he had
planned.

After making a long series of studies of the selective
absorption of the earth's atmosphere at the lower levels or
valleys, he planned in 1881 to make a similar investigation

on the top of Mount Whitney in Southern California. In preparation for this expedition I had to do a piece of work in silvering for him which had possibly never been undertaken before, that is, to get a perfect surface from the solution or bath without any retouching whatever. He purchased chemicals of extraordinary purity for me in New York, and I succeeded very well indeed. I made for him also a long telescope with which he proposed to try to see the solar corona without a total solar eclipse, the object of the long tube being to eliminate all other light but the light from the sun and the corona alone. He wrote me afterwards that he made a failure of seeing the corona from the carelessness or wickedness or what not of a soldier who, so the story goes, saw a little dust on the mirror and took his handkerchief to rub it off! The sequel may easily be imagined. But the other results of the Mount Whitney expedition have now become classic; indeed, to a large degree they have settled the problem of the selective absorption of the earth's atmosphere in its relations to the sun's radiant energy and the intimately correlated problem of life upon our globe.

In 1886, just after we had moved my shop to Allegheny near the old Observatory, Professor Langley became assistant secretary of the Smithsonian Institution at Washington, still retaining his position at the Observatory. The following year, upon the death of Professor Baird, he was called to the secretaryship of the Institution, the highest position in any scientific institution in the land. He was an indefatigable worker and deserved all the honor and success which came to him. This great honor came just at the time when, through Mr. Thaw's liberality, he had constructed apparatus to begin his famous researches in aerodynamics at the Observatory, and the Smithsonian Institution made arrangements whereby he could retain the directorship of the Observatory for a while and spend some time there. At that time I can remember he had a whirling machine on which he suspended birds, wheels, and frictionless planes of various sorts, with which he made experiments to discover their resistances, the action of the air upon them, etc.

For three years I was associated with Professor Langley in his investigations of the great problem of flight. The story of how he became interested in this problem is a long one, but suffice it to say that his original purpose was not to construct a flying machine, but to determine, if possible, the laws governing flight. He undertook to solve this most fascinating problem in his usual rigorously scientific manner. He always commenced at the bottom and worked right straight up.

Much of the apparatus for these investigations was made in our shops. He would make sketches and tell me what he wanted and I would work out the mechanical problems involved and supply the apparatus.[1] His assistant, Professor Very, carried on the researches at the Observatory after Langley had moved to Washington, and we made apparatus for him, too. After 1890, however, Langley's researches in flight were carried on largely in Washington. In May, 1896, his steam-driven aerodrome model, launched by a catapult which shot it off the roof of a houseboat on the Potomac, made a beautiful,

---

[1] See Appendix for Langley's autograph order to Brashear, dated March 8, 1887, for an experimental airplane model with a 5-ft. by 6-in. wing.

steady flight, and, gliding gracefully down, alighted
gently on the water none the worse for its trip except for
a wetting. That flight convinced a hitherto skeptical
world of the practicability of mechanical flight, and at a
later period Langley himself said:

I have brought to a close the portion of the work which
seemed to be specially mine: the demonstration of the practicability of mechanical flight. For the next stage, which is the
commercial and practical development of the idea, it is probable
that the world may look to others. . . . The great universal
highway overhead is now soon to be opened.

In 1903, just as he had reached the point of success with
his man-carrying flying machine, the failure of one part
of the mechanism wrecked it. It wrecked my dear friend's
hopes, too, and the unkindly comments of the press over-
whelmed him. He passed from this earth in 1906, feeling
in many ways that his life-work had been a failure, but
the successful work in aviation since then has been based
upon Langley's pioneer investigations.

I can never forget the generous help given me in the
solution of optical problems from the very beginning of
my acquaintanceship with Professor Langley. I never
visited the Smithsonian Institution while he was there
that he did not call to my mind that first night we met,
when, with fear and trembling, I unwrapped from a red
bandana handkerchief my first five-inch objective which
my wife and I had made. His encouragement then and
afterwards made my subsequent work easier by far. Our
friendship remained unbroken. I remember how he used
to sit in the Observatory and read to me of an evening
from the manuscript of his book on "The New Astronomy." What beautiful thoughts, what charming de-

scriptions, it contains! Of an afternoon he would come over to my shop to watch the baseball games, as the park was in sight and a telescopic view of the game very satisfactory.

I loved Professor Langley as a friend — aye, as a brother — and I treasure letters from him which speak of his true affection for me. I humbly pay my tribute here to this master investigator who solved so many of the mysteries of the universe.

CHAPTER XV

THE NEW ALLEGHENY OBSERVATORY

MY memories regarding the history of the Allegheny Observatory and the men who have been associated in its development and its researches are all very dear to me. During Langley's directorship, Messrs. Frost, Hall, Very, and Keeler were all associated with him. Since that time each has made for himself an honored record. Professor Keeler left us in 1886 to have charge of the erection of the instruments and install the apparatus for the time service at the Lick Observatory. After Professor Holden took charge of the Lick Observatory, Keeler was appointed astronomer. He soon developed the astronomical spectroscope to a high degree of perfection and made a series of observations on the motion of the nebulæ in the line of sight which at once brought his work the highest recognition in the scientific world. His magnificent drawings of the planets Jupiter, Saturn, and Mars, made by the aid of the great thirty-six-inch telescope, have never been surpassed. Many other studies of importance were conducted at the Observatory which placed Keeler among the most earnest and successful observers in the realm of the new astronomy.

When Langley left the Allegheny Observatory to become secretary of the Smithsonian Institution, Professor Keeler was unanimously elected to the directorship (May,

1891), a position he at once accepted. He found our Observatory poorly equipped for the line of investigation he desired to pursue as a continuation of his work at Lick Observatory, but friends of the institution and of Keeler soon furnished the means for some new apparatus. Mrs. William Thaw contributed the money to construct a spectroscope of the highest type, designed by Keeler. William Thaw, Jr., supplied the means for a new driving clock and the remounting of the thirteen-inch equatorial, while the Junta Club of Pittsburgh generously donated a sum sufficient to place a modern shutter on the dome. Thus equipped, Keeler commenced a series of researches by which, in the years he was with us, some of the most brilliant discoveries ever made in astronomical science were added to those he had already given to the world.

But the site of the old Observatory was fast becoming about hopeless for further work on account of the increase in the consumption of soft coal in the vicinity. By the early nineties it was completely surrounded with homes. In 1894 I was elected chairman of the Allegheny Observatory Committee of the University of Pittsburgh (then the Western University of Pennsylvania), a position I still hold as I pen these lines. At just about this time the citizens of Allegheny purchased the property of the Watson farm lying south of Perrysville Road. As I was a subscriber to the fund with which the purchase was made, I worked for the purpose of securing a site for a new observatory on a beautiful hilltop in the middle of Riverview Park, as the plot was called, and was successful. The Citizens' Committee reserved the tract, set it aside to be used for the proposed observatory, and further provided that no buildings should be placed near it.

The location thus secured was as admirable as could be found anywhere in the western part of Pennsylvania. The hill is the highest but one in the State, west of the Laurel Ridge. It commanded a glorious view for many miles down the Ohio valley, and was so situated that prevailing winds carried the smoke of the cities away from the proposed observatory, forever preventing the presence of the smoke nuisance which for years created almost insuperable difficulties for Professors Langley and Keeler in their scientific work. There was a quality in the atmosphere of the spot which made it especially adapted for solar observations. In fact, it was one of the best places in the country for an observatory.

With the site secured, I then started to see what could be done about raising money to build and equip the Observatory, and found that it was useless to push the matter as, due to the financial panic of 1893, times were "hard." I talked the situation over with Mr. Carnegie, who advised me not to do anything until times were better, and I well remember he said, "Wait, Brashear, until coke sells at a dollar a ton and we will build the Observatory."

So, for the time being, I gave up pushing the project. Keeler and I, however, worked up drawings, plans, etc., and developed the general features of the proposed plant. Keeler, with the meager and antiquated equipment of the old Observatory, continued his investigations and made such marvelous discoveries that he was considered the peer of any astronomer in the world. But he was rapidly approaching the "end of his string" until he had new resources. Socially he was a most charming man, and as a scientific investigator he was of the highest type, ever ready, ever willing to help the earnest student over the rough ways that here and there lay before him. Thousands of people enjoyed his Thursday night receptions at the Observatory, and he was one of the first to suggest that when we had a new Observatory one department should be erected to be forever free to the people so that they too might enjoy the beauties of the skies.

Early in 1898 Keeler was offered a position in charge of stellar spectroscopy at the Yerkes Observatory. Within a week or so he was offered the directorship of the Lick Observatory, to take the place made vacant by the resignation of Professor Holden. Notwithstanding those proffered honors, he did not want to leave us, so deeply had he become interested in and associated with the scientific work in Pittsburgh. But he recognized his duty to science as well as to himself, and decided that unless Pittsburgh could assure him an equipment commensurate with the problems that awaited solution in the domain of the new astronomy, he must accept the Lick directorship where he could continue his valuable work. Accordingly, he set a time limit for his acceptance or refusal of the Lick offer.

I started almost single-handed to raise the money, if possible, for the new Observatory, with no assistance from any member of the Board of Trustees of the Observatory. While I stated in all my correspondence and interviews that we wanted to keep Professor Keeler, I put the project on the much broader basis of erecting a build-

ing and obtaining an equipment that would be a source of
civic pride and would retain the prestige given to our
good old Observatory by Professor Langley and his
successor.

The breaking-out of the Spanish-American War and
the excitement associated with it helped to prevent the
successful completion of the task I had undertaken. Several large subscriptions were made and many smaller ones,
but the results were not what I had so ardently hoped for.
The aggregate of the subscriptions fell short of one hundred and fifty thousand dollars, or less than three fourths
of the required sum. My seven weeks' hard labor of love
did not succeed. Keeler hesitated as long as he could with
courtesy to the Lick trustees, and accepted the position
only when the time limit had been reached.

The short time (two and a half years) that he spent as
the director of the great mountain observatory was replete
with success. After a year of unremitting labor with the
Crossley reflector, he gave to the world the most magnificent photographs of the nebulæ ever produced. He wrote
me: "I have just sent an article to the *Nachrichten* which
describes what is, I think, the best discovery I have made
yet, namely, that the majority of the nebulæ are spirals,
and that the spiral form is that which is usually or normally assumed by nebulæ in the process of condensation.
I have estimated that there are not less than 100,000
nebulæ in the sky within the range of the Crossley reflector."

Since that letter was written his monographs on the
subject have been published in the "Astrophysical Journal," clearly written, as is characteristic of all his papers,

for Keeler wielded a facile pen. His descriptions were wonderfully clear and charming, his logic always clean-cut.

His health, however, did not thrive in the altitude of Mount Hamilton under the strenuous night work which he chose and pursued with such enthusiasm and success, and he left us on August 13, 1900.

> Death makes no conquest of the conqueror,
> For now he lives in fame, though not in life.

After Keeler's resignation, which took effect on May 1, 1898, at the request of the Observatory Committee I consented to serve as Acting Director until the question of the new Observatory was settled. This position I retained for eighteen months, when Professor F. L. O. Wadsworth was unanimously elected to take the place vacated by Keeler. For a short while after Keeler's resignation I did not push the work of raising further subscriptions. It was unfortunate for us that some of the subscriptions had been given on the basis of Keeler's staying with us. However, when the work was again taken up, hundreds of letters and circulars were sent out and I had many personal interviews with people interested in the Observatory project, and practically all the money which had been subscribed in the early months of 1898 was secured, together with enough new subscriptions to warrant our going ahead.

Professor Keeler's original plans were modified and made more complete by Professor Wadsworth, who contributed his time and valuable ideas generously. The Observatory Committee gave much assistance and advice. The plans were given out for competitive architectural designs for the new building, and among the architects who submitted designs, T. E. Billquest was chosen.

Saturday afternoon, October 20, 1900, was chosen for laying the nearest thing to a "corner" stone in a building to consist of three round towers surmounted by hemispherical domes. But it was not for twelve more years that the building and equipment were sufficiently advanced to warrant their dedication and presentation to the University.

Those twelve years were busy ones for me. In 1901 some of my "outside" duties were as Acting Chancellor and member of the Board of Trustees of the Western University of Pennsylvania, chairman of the Observatory Committee, member of the Carnegie Institute, including the Carnegie Museum Committee and the Plan and Scope Committee for the Carnegie Technical Schools that were soon to be built (a position requiring a vast expenditure of time and energy), member of the Sanitation Committee, member and Councillor of the Academy of Science, and a member of various engineering and scientific societies and literary clubs both at home and abroad. In addition Mrs. Brashear was in poor health, practically an invalid, and we had almost more work than we could handle at the shops. I was burdened almost beyond endurance and felt that I must throw off some of my extra duties, but somehow I always found it easier to assume new responsibilities than to discard them when they were once taken on. I suspect I should be very unhappy if I had nothing but my business to look after. In the press of all my work, it became apparent that we did not have sufficient funds to complete the Observatory. In 1905, ten days before I was to take Mrs. Brashear to Muskoka for the summer in the hope that it might be of benefit to her, I was invited to take dinner with my friend Mr. H. C. Frick to discuss with him the raising of sufficient funds to complete the new Observatory. To make a long story short, Mr. Frick said, "Brashear, go and find out what it will cost to finish the building and equipment and I will give you half the amount if you will raise the balance by October 15th."

It meant a whole summer's work for "Brashear," but there was no backing out. Before I left for Muskoka I learned that it would require $65,000 to finish everything needed, which meant that I had to raise $32,500 at "long distance" — not an easy job. I took up the work as soon as we were settled. It would have been easy enough to attend to correspondence, but my wife was so poorly all that summer that I worked under much stress, though she kept good heart and held up bravely when I knew she was suffering all the time.

When we reached home the middle of September I had secured about $20,000. In the month that remained I had to hustle, but I "had to get that woodchuck," and get it I did, with a few thousands for good measure.

This was in 1905, but it was not until 1912 that the dedication of the building and equipment occurred. The Astronomical and Astrophysical Society of America had accepted an invitation to hold its August, 1912, meeting in Pittsburgh, and it was decided to have the dedicatory exercises of the Observatory in the presence of the Society on Wednesday afternoon, August 28th. It was with a full heart that, as chairman of the Observatory Committee, I made the address presenting the new Allegheny Observatory to the Trustees of the University of Pittsburgh, a building dedicated to the cause of pure science and to the cause of popular intelligence, in which every nook and corner was suited to carrying out some problem in the new astronomy of which such vast fields are still unexplored.

Nearly $300,000 was subscribed to build and equip the new Observatory. Part of it was given for special purposes. A fund was given by the friends of Professor Keeler to erect a thirty-inch reflecting telescope to his memory. The great refractor under the dome in which the dedicatory exercises were held was the gift of the immediate families of William Thaw and of William Thaw, Jr. I cannot pass on here without mentioning again the interest of these two men in the work of Professors Langley and Keeler. Other citizens of Pittsburgh were interested in this work too, but these two men, one directly interested in the work of Langley, the other more especially in that of Keeler, were mighty factors in their interest and helpfulness in the old Observatory. The delightful association of William Thaw, Jr., with Keeler in his researches and epoch-making discoveries in the domain of astrophysics was, alas, cut short by the passing away of Mr. Thaw in Europe in 1892, just three years after the death of his father. The family and friends of Mr. Thaw, father and son, helped nobly in bringing the work of building and equipping the new Observatory to completion.

I cannot refrain from referring to the names of Miss Jennie and Miss Mathilda Smith, two good women that lived on the avenue just beyond the Observatory, who, from the very beginning of the work on the new institution, contributed liberally, not only of their means, but gave their personal interest to many of the details of architecture, ornamentation, and other things. A beautiful window on the northern side of the building, the Riefler precision clock, the beautiful marble finish of the main building, and many other such matters were due to their interest and generosity. They have both passed over to the other side, but their works remain.

Henry Kirke Porter, a warm personal friend of Keeler's, was responsible for the great solar spectrograph which is part of the equipment of the Keeler Memorial. Charles Schwab, when I went to see him about getting reasonable terms on the construction steel, ended the interview by giving an order to his secretary to have all the steel for the Observatory building proper charged to his personal account. But there are so many names on the roll of honor of those who contributed generously to the new Observatory that I must not attempt to name them all. One more happy story I must tell, though.

In my early struggles to gain a knowledge of the stars, I made a resolution that if ever an opportunity offered or I could make such an opportunity, I should have a place where all the people who loved the stars could enjoy them; and I am delighted to say that through the generosity of Mr. and Mrs. Robert C. Hall the new Observatory contains a beautiful lecture room that is forever free to the people, where lectures and illustrations of astronomical subjects are given by the staff of the Observatory; and the dear old thirteen-inch telescope, by the use of which so many discoveries were made, is also given up to the use of the citizens of Pittsburgh, or, for that matter, citizens of the world. Thousands upon thousands of visitors have taken advantage of this free department, and do you think that kind of people will get into riots or fights or anything of the sort? I tell you there is nothing that I know of that contributes more to the elevating and the ennobling of the human and the spiritual in man than to see something of God's beautiful work.

Mr. Frick set aside a fund for the endowment of this department. Night after night the Observatory is open, and if it rains visitors do not have to go without a recompense; for fine lantern slides showing the beauties of the heavens have been provided, which are projected upon the screen and a little talk or lecture about them is given. School children of advanced age are encouraged to study. No distinction is made between Catholic or Protestant, between Jew or Gentile.

I think I have failed to mention that in 1905 Dr. Frank Schlesinger succeeded Professor Wadsworth as Director of the Observatory. I have no hesitancy in saying that we have reason to be proud of the contributions to our loved science that have gone out from our new institution under his most able and efficient direction.

What gratitude I felt that I had lived to see the auspicious day when this "temple of the skies," so long dreamed about, planned, and worked for, should finally be achieved! My heart turned to my fellow workmen in the little workshop on the hill who had done so much to make the instrumental equipment a success, especially to my son-in-law McDowell who had left no stone unturned that we might have the very best. But the day of fulfillment was saddened for me because that kindly and beautiful spirit of her who had been my help and inspiration through so many of my struggles was no longer with me to share the joys of the work we had accomplished together.

CHAPTER XVI
LIFE AT MUSKOKA

UP until the time I was fifty-five, I think I never had a decent vacation, one when I could really rest without having a boiled shirt handy. In 1896 Ma and I first went to Muskoka Lakes, Canada. It was a sad year for us. Our boy Harry had returned home from his vacation very sick, developed typhoid fever, and after a month's illness passed away. We had a trained nurse, but he never wanted Ma out of his sight, and she never left him. Weary and worn out with her long watching, she made a misstep in going downstairs, and in falling broke the fibula in four places and smashed her ankle so badly that she was crippled for the rest of her life. It was a hard task to get her to the Lakes that summer, but I am sure it saved her life.

After renting a cottage there for three summers, we finally concluded to buy one of the small islands for ourselves. McDowell was such a power in the workshop that I felt a certain degree of freedom about going away for a month or two at a time. Indeed, I must give him the credit for a large part of the success of the firm. He is a master in the optical line and stops at nothing that is at all possible.

After we had determined to buy at Muskoka, we had a lot of trouble before we got hold of just what we wanted.

The Lakes are about thirty miles in extent in their various directions, and contain about eight hundred islands. Owing to the island boundaries you cannot see more than five miles in any direction, and as you sail along new vistas open up, and much of the beauty lies in these ever-changing features.

At last we found our island, Isle Urania. Its sylvan and lake attractions make it a veritable paradise without the flaming sword. We built a cottage and a boathouse, and I don't know how I should get through the year's work any more without this charming retreat. The air is so pure, quite equal to ocean air, as often it comes over the Great Lakes to the west of us through twenty miles of pines and cedars; and everything is conducive to building one up. The waters of Muskoka seem to be a panacea for many troubles. There is not a bit of lime in it. It is strange that, up until a short time before we started to go there, Muskoka was not known as a health-giving summer resort, but simply as a great lumber region.

We feel about our Isle Urania much as the fellow felt when he said, "God might have made a better berry than the strawberry, but he didn't." There may be a prettier place than Muskoka in the world, but in all my travels I have never come across it. I have heard of the Italian lakes, have seen the Swiss lakes, and many of the lakes in our own country — Lake Champlain, Lake George, and the Great Lakes — but for wild natural scenery no place has yet reached the wonderful charm of Muskoka as an ideal summer spot, free, largely free, from the environ-ments of conventional city life. To my mind the Hawaiian Islands come nearest to it. It is in the Laurentian geologic region, and the glaciers of probably a million years ago or more cut out the basins where the Lakes now find a home. It is one of the wonders of Nature that ice could have done such mighty work.

There are several glacier boulders on our island, the monster boulder being just back of the veranda. I have measured it as carefully as I could, and I find its weight to be 180 tons, or 360,000 pounds. There is one boulder on the mainland that surely weighs 500 tons. They are all of hard granitic schist, with seams of quartzite sometimes a foot wide and extending for hundreds of yards. Most of them are colored a reddish brown, and I have been told by an official of the United States Coast and Geodetic Survey that the seams all contain gold, but not in sufficient quantities to make its removal a paying proposition.

But, alas, we hardly find perfection in anything. Muskoka sometimes suffers from long periods of drought (only three or four times in the twenty-odd summers I have been going there) which brings with it forest fires of a most direful and destructive nature. One summer, just two hundred miles north of us, hundreds were driven into the Lake to protect themselves from the destroying fires that raged around them. Animals, from wild bear and deer to the red squirrel, had to seek the Lake for refuge. Sometimes the fires were much nearer us. Once we could see the flames extending for nearly two miles, and that end of the burning brush, as they call it, was not over two miles from us. You can imagine how everybody in the region was made happy when the rain came at last and stifled the flames.

In those early days at Muskoka we had a couple of sail-boats and three rowboats, one of which I had made especially for Mrs. Brashear. She was very fond of being on the water, but was rather afraid in a sailboat, and on account of her accident it was hard for her to be comfortable in an ordinary rowboat. Early in 1901 I ordered a little steam launch, thirty-four feet long, for her especial pleasure. It was built under my special directions by the Davis Dry Dock Company at Kingston. We had finished paying for our cottage — and, by the way, we paid every dollar on that cottage with money I earned by lecturing and other work outside the little workshop — and had decided on a way to pay for the launch. We had a small fund we had saved for another trip to Europe, but in Ma's crippled condition we both knew such a trip was out of the question, so we thought that by investing this fund in an island at Muskoka which was offered to us by an old Canadian friend at a low figure, we could dispose of it at a profit big enough to pay for the launch.

Well, I had ordered the launch when, like a stroke of lightning, my friend Mr. Henry W. Oliver, who, so far as I knew, did not know I was even interested in a launch, asked my permission to present us with one for our summer house at Muskoka! His offer was made in such a generous spirit of human kindness as an appreciation of my life-work that I could not but say yes. Here was another friend like Mr. Thaw, Mr. Phipps, Mr. Carnegie, Mr. Frick, and so many others, come to make my life happier, and more, to make happy the dear one who had then stood by me for nearly forty years, and who had done so much to make my life-work a success. Scientific men owe much to men like these for the beautiful spirit they have shown in their very generous gifts, made "not for charity, but as a recognition of a life-work so often done without proper monetary compensation."

No boat on the Muskoka Lakes was better adapted for the pleasure of a family than ours, and few, if any, had such graceful lines. Mr. Kuhn's Lady of the Lake might have come near it, but I liked our Alleghenia best. Her speed was nine and one-half miles an hour — ten miles if forced. Steam could be raised easily in twenty minutes, and if in a hurry in fifteen. Her engines were compound non-condensing; her length thirty-four feet, beam seven feet. In the three summers we used her we traveled about twenty-seven hundred miles.

One day — it was in the summer of 1903 — we made a trip to Gravenhurst, returning about three o'clock against a very heavy wind and boisterous sea. The young man who had been running the engine kept a stick or two of wood under the boiler, but as we did not go for the mail that evening no steam was raised. We frequently had incipient fires around the firebox — the wood catching when the fire had been going two or three hours — so we always looked carefully to see if everything was all right before we left the boat, and everything was apparently all right on this particular day.

About eleven-forty-five we were awakened by a cry of "Fire" from a neighbor who had seen our boat burning and who had crossed in his boat to waken us. I hastily donned a few clothes, grabbed a chemical fire extinguisher I always kept handy, and rushed to the dock. My good neighbor had put out the roof-deck fire except around the boiler stack, so I put the fire extinguisher to work in the hold and with difficulty succeeded in keeping the boat from sinking. The fire had caught under the floor on the starboard side and had burned about two by three feet of the hull, and set fire to the seats and cushions. The machinery was not in any way injured.

The occurrence was quite a shock to Ma, who had been very ill that summer with an incipient paralysis of the tongue and other complications which had all but taken her life. Her affection for the little craft was almost like that for a child. We could not bear the thought of giving it up, so we decided to have new planks put in the burned place and all the woodwork that was injured replaced. We also had a little more steaming capacity put into the boiler and had it made safe from fire.

We should have been able to use the boat comfortably for years — indeed, we planned to do so — but Mr. Carnegie, when he heard of the accident to the Alleghenia, presented us with a new boat similar to the last one, but bigger and better, one that traveled more smoothly in the rough waters for which Muskoka is famous. This boat was designed even more carefully for Ma's comfort and was named for her, Phœbe. It was completed for our use for the summer of 1904. How I hoped that my dear companion would live to enjoy this little boat as she did the other one! It seemed that when I could give her any comfort or happiness by word or deed, it came back with redoubled energy to me, and her pleasure in the new boat was beautiful to see. For a few summers more we enjoyed our beloved Muskoka together, and then one day on our beautiful Isle of Urania, like the sinking of a summer sun that sweet spirit left me. It was on September 23, 1910, just a couple of months after my mother, too, had gone over to the Summer Land.

So many kindly letters of affection and sympathy came to me after her dear life had gone out that I found it impossible to acknowledge all of them, as I should like to have done, and the thought came to me to send all these friends a copy of a poem by my friend Albert Bigelow Paine, the friend and biographer of Mark Twain, whom I also had the honor to know and love. My dear wife was so fond of the poem that I thought nothing I could say would be nearer to my thoughts of her.

Folded Hands

Poor, tired hands that toiled so hard for me,
  At rest before me now I see them lying.
They toiled so hard; and yet we could not see
  That she was dying.

Poor, tired hands that drudged the livelong day,
  Still busy when the midnight oil was burning;
Oft toiling on until she saw the gray
  Of day returning.

If I could sit and hold those tired hands,
  And feel the warm life-blood within them beating,
And gaze with her across the twilight lands,
  Some whispered words repeating:

I know to-night that I would love her so,
  And I could tell my love to her so truly,
That e'en though tired, she would not wish to go
  And leave me here so lonely.

Poor, tired heart that had so weary grown,
  That death came all unheeded o'er it creeping,
How sad it is to sit here all alone,
  While she is sleeping.

> Dear, patient heart that deemed the heavy care
>   Of drudging household toil its highest duty;
> That laid aside its precious yearnings there
>   Along with beauty.
>
> Dear heart and hands, so pulseless, still, and cold,
>   (How peacefully and dreamlessly she's sleeping,)
> The spotless shroud of rest about them fold,
>   And leave me weeping.

After the dear one had passed away, by mutual understanding her remains were cremated, and I placed the ashes in the urn with my own hands, and laid them away in the columbarium under the dome of the new Allegheny Observatory to which I had given so many years of my life.

On the marble slab that covers the urn containing the ashes I have had engraved these lines taken from an anonymous poem I came across in my early life, and expressing as I could not do the real, the vital principle of our life-work:

> We have loved the stars too fondly
> To be fearful of the night.

Muskoka became a different place after her dear light went out, but long before this there had been new generations coming on and the young people in my house added new interests in life for me. We continued to spend our summers in the "King's Dominions" and often have our good friends with us. The flowers are just as lovely each spring as they were the year before, flox, snapdragon, petunias, goldenglow, and sweet alyssum; and the fishing — but I won't stop to tell any fish stories here. The early days, however, when we ate off a box, slept on the floor, washed in a pudding pan, and stirred our tea and coffee with a sliver off a shingle while we were getting things opened up and going for the season, still afford me moments of vivid memories. It was as near camping as anything could be.

Here I must stop to record the sad story of the burning of the Phœbe. I was in California in November, 1913, when I received word that Tom Robinson's boathouse, in which the little steamer had been put for the winter, had caught fire and in the conflagration which followed the Phœbe had been burned. I was all broken up for a while about it, but when I came home I was astonished to find that the many dear friends who go to Muskoka every year and who always called the little steamboat the Good Samaritan, had gotten together unknown to me and subscribed five thousand dollars to build a new boat and boathouse for me. So now, when my friends come to Muskoka the new Phœbe meets them oftentimes at Gravenhurst to carry them up the lake to our modest cottage where city cares are left behind.

In my summer trips to Canada I frequently give illustrated lectures for the benefit of the Children's Hospital of Toronto, the Ladies' Aid Societies, Canadian Clubs, and in later years for the benefit of all kinds of war activities. I am not a lecturer. That is not my business. But hundreds and hundreds of times I have told the story of the good and beautiful things that have come into my life, for, after all, it is sharing the good I have received with the "other fellow" that makes life worth living. Sometimes I wonder at the problems presented to me in my audiences. At our settlement houses in the slums I often address crowds of foreigners of a low type, and somehow

I seem to have no trouble to get into the hearts of these people. It seems a gift God gave me long, long ago. Too many forget that there is always some one in such a motley crowd that is hungry for a part of the beautiful truth of nature, and if in the midst of a busy life I can give it to them I am more than repaid for my labor.

Carlyle says somewhere in "Sartor Resartus," "That there should one man die ignorant who had capacity for knowledge, this I call a tragedy." How deep with meaning these words are! For more than fifty years I have done what I could to send out sweetness and light into the dark places of our cities. But I sometimes think there is a little touch of selfishness back of it, for none of us can do a kindly act or say a helpful word but it brings back to us a big percentage of interest.

I shall never forget once when I went out to the State prison to talk with the unfortunate inmates about Halley's Comet. I used to go out a couple of times a year to talk with them. This time I found in the reception room fourteen telescopes (?) they had made with the hope of catching a glimpse of the comet through the bars of the prison. They had made a paste of the bread given them, and, taking strips of newspaper, had made odd-looking tubes by pasting strips diagonally, or, better, spirally over broom handles, and then had in some manner secured long-focus spectacle lenses to put in each end of the tube. They were practically worthless, but they showed a real desire in some of the prisoners to see some of God's handiwork.

I never think of this without remembering a saying I heard many years ago: "Show me the best man in the world and I will show you some little desert spot in his nature. Show me the worst man in the world and I will find some little green oasis there."

I had, of course, a little telescope to use at Muskoka. It was mounted on a tripod on the porch of the cottage, and people used to come in their boats on fine nights to get a peep at whatever could be seen. Lovelier nights never came than some I can remember on Urania with the moon and the monarch Jupiter throwing their beautiful light over the Lake. The nights at times were clear as a bell, perfect for observation as we would catch the thin crescent of the new moon just as it was ready to go behind a tree and then behind the hill. Sometimes I would show my little audience the motion of the earth on its axis by a few minutes' watching without the aid of the telescope. But the greatest pleasure I had in sky-gazing there was in watching the Aurora Borealis which gave a more beautiful spectacle at Muskoka than it gave at any other place in the world that I ever saw. I can remember that some nights after I had gone to bed I could not stand it and would drag some bedclothes out on the veranda and lie watching the wonderful lights for hours. What a blessing it is that wherever we are the beauty of God's universe is ever with us!

CHAPTER XVII
EDUCATIONAL ACTIVITIES

In 1900, Dr. W. J. Holland was elected Director of the Carnegie Museum and tendered his resignation as Chancellor of the Western University of Pennsylvania. A committee, consisting of Dr. John C. White, A. W. Mellon, William McConway, Judge J. H. Reed, W. J. Sawyer, and myself, was appointed to find and present nominations for a new chancellor.

In the course of the next year I absolutely refused *three* times to accept the position of Acting Chancellor to serve until we could find just the right man for the position.

The faculty and alumni of the University almost got down on their knees to ask me to help them over the "slough of despond" they were in, and the boys who were in school — well, they gave me a great ovation when in May, 1901, I first went over to the University after I had expressed a willingness to see what I could do for them.

From the beginning I urged upon the Trustees the paramount importance of finding the right man, an administrator and a scholar, to devote all his time and energy to the building-up of the great university. At the end of three years that man had not been found, but I found my health breaking down under the strain of the many duties I had assumed, and, as a relief from some of

156

my burdens, I resigned from the Acting Chancellorship. I think in those three years of "working together" we had a good measure of success, and when I left, the University was in a prosperous condition.

In severing my connection as Acting Chancellor, I retained my membership on the Board of Trustees. I could not think of entirely withdrawing from my associations with the University with which I had been more or less intimately connected for more than twenty-five years, as long as I could be of any slight use in furthering her interests.

This period of work overlapped the beginning of my work for the Carnegie Institute of Technology. Up to this time Mr. Carnegie had done great things for England and Scotland as well as for America. He certainly had been a "record-breaker" in the way of giving money for libraries and educational institutions. He had given me twenty thousand dollars for the new Allegheny Observatory which was well on its way. But the big project he had in his mind at this time was the creation of a Technical School where it would be possible for any worthy youth to obtain an education to fit him for his life's work. On November 15, 1900, he wrote the following enthusiastic letter to the Mayor of Pittsburgh:

I learn with deep interest that the Central Board of Education has asked the City of Pittsburgh for $100,000 to begin a technical school, no doubt to obtain for the bright youth of the high school the essential advantages which technical education in our day affords.

For many years I have nursed the pleasant thought that I might be the fortunate giver of a Technical Institute to our city fashioned upon the best models, for I know of no institution which Pittsburgh, as an industrial center, so much needs.

I postponed moving in the matter because I wished the Carnegie Institute (whose first building was originally intended to unite under its roof the Academy of Science and Art and other scientific and technical societies, as well as the central library) to be fairly launched upon its new development before drawing the attention of Pittsburgh to the Technical Institute. The action of the Education Board, however, impels me to step forward now and ask that I may be allowed to do what I have long wished to do for Pittsburgh.

I have given much attention to technical schools both in the United States and Great Britain during the past few years. The work now being done by the Technical Institutes in Boston and Worcester, the Drexel Institute in Philadelphia, the Pratt Institute in Brooklyn, and the Armour Institute in Chicago, is most encouraging. . . .

It is really astonishing how many of the world's foremost men have begun as manual laborers. The greatest of all, Shakespeare, was a woolcarder; Burns, a plowman; Columbus, a sailor; Hannibal, a blacksmith; Lincoln, a rail-splitter; Grant, a tanner. I know of no better foundation from which to ascend than manual labor in youth.

We have two notable examples of this in our own community, whose fame is world-wide. George Westinghouse was a mechanic; Professor Brashear a millwright.

I believe that a first-class technical school, probably as large as that of Worcester, would develop latent talent around us to such an extent as to surprise the most sanguine.

If the City of Pittsburgh will furnish a site, which I hope will be of ample size for future extensions, I shall be delighted to provide the money for such a school, taking care to provide room for additions to the buildings, to meet the certain growth of Pittsburgh.

I would endow it with $1,000,000 in five-per-cent gold bonds, yielding a revenue of $50,000 per year.

The rare ability with which the Trustees of the Carnegie Institute have managed it, and the results which have so surprised and gratified me, naturally lead me to beg these gentlemen to take charge of the Technical Institute and its endowment.

The City Councils of Pittsburgh accepted this generous offer and proceeded to secure a site for the Technical School in accordance with the conditions of the gift.

In the mean time a Committee of Carnegie Institute was appointed. There were but three of us — William McConway, Charles M. Schwab, and myself. The task was a big one, but we were all deeply interested in it, though it took a great deal of time to do the work that had to be done. I personally spent many weeks, even months, in the development of the great scheme for the school and I know the other members of the Committee did the same. The selection of a site proved a difficult matter. It seemed to me that we needed plenty of room to spread. I had visited more than a dozen technical schools in this country and abroad, and every one of them was crying for more room — some were even building additions which shut out the light from other buildings so that artificial light had to be used constantly. We finally secured the site on which the school is now located.

The first report of our Committee Mr. Carnegie considered too ambitious. A much more modest scheme was proposed, and this became the basis for the Carnegie Institute of Technology. On the first advisory committee were some very good men, among them Dr. Robert H. Thurston, of Cornell University, who submitted the first report in which some of the recommendations were considered too advanced at the time, but which were subsequently adopted with Mr. Carnegie's full approval.

Among other things Professor Thurston advised not less than thirty square feet per student in classrooms; in drawing rooms about one hundred, and in laboratories from one hundred and fifty to five hundred feet according to the character of the work to be done and magnitude of the space required for machinery and apparatus.

Is it practicable [Professor Thurston asked] to carry into effect that ambition of every technical educator, so admirably pictured by Scott Russell's "The Technical University," on the lines of which Ezra Cornell would have approved, where every man could secure instruction in any study in such departments as are capable of being utilized practicably in the sequel of life? It is obvious that could such an institution be founded, and thus the whole example be furnished in full perfection and a standard thus provided by which to measure, the establishment of this complete and perfect model would, very probably, advance the cause of useful education of the people for the life and work of the people for many years. It is possible that the opportunity is here and now presented, and that, lost, it may not recur again. . . .

As to the higher departments of the new school, Professor Thurston expressed himself most charmingly in the language of John Russell on the occasion of the latter's visit to a German technical university:

A technical university abroad was to me a surprise, a profound lesson, a delight. It was a dream of my youth suddenly embodied in living substance, and, unlike other realized dreams, the reality exceeded the fiction. It was one of my early dreams that highly educated men should engage in teaching skilled workmen the profound philosophical principles which underlie all material work, and I hoped so to make their work their pleasure, excellence their ultimate aim, and truth of execution and perfection of finish their highest ambition.

Every division of the institution, from lowest to highest and first to last, should be so planned as to work in concert with the public schools of similar grade as far as practicable. . . . The technical school would be able, in some cases probably, to promote the initiation of special instruction in manual training and in the kindergarten forms of technical work in the public schools. Every possible means of allying the technical and the common school work should be availed of, and the cardinal principle should be constantly proclaimed and enforced. The purpose of the whole movement is to advance the best interests of the people of Pittsburgh and its vicinity. It should be distinctly understood that it is desired to make use of all possible ways to that end and to coöperate with every other educational movement.

My duties for the school were somewhat lightened after we had our Director. I told Mr. Carnegie that if I were a good Presbyterian I would say the Lord made and saved Arthur Hamerschlag for this great work. He certainly proved himself to be a marvelous hustler.

We broke ground for the first building on the 3d of August, 1905. On October 21st we had about four hundred students, if I remember rightly, and before the winter was over we had more than seven hundred. Additional buildings were completed, and then we built a large department for the women's school. But the growth of this marvelous institution is too well known to need recording here. Mr. Carnegie multiplied his original gift time after time, and his conception of the ultimate scope of the school, which was necessarily rather limited and indefinite at first, grew rapidly until the Institute took the marvelous place among technical schools that it now occupies.

One day in July, 1909, while I was in Muskoka trying to nurse Ma back to health, I received an unexpected letter from F. W. McElroy, Mr. Frick's personal representative in Pittsburgh, stating that Mr. Frick wanted to see me at his summer home at Pride's Crossing, Massachusetts, on the 28th. On account of Ma's illness, I could

not fulfill his request until early in August. I reached
Pride's Crossing on August 4th, and had a most hospitable
reception. The room Mr. Frick's daughter Helen took
me to was almost as big as the whole lower floor of our
Muskoka cottage. The walls were covered with silk
damask. The beds were of mahogany and finest down.
A window opened right on the sea. Below me I could
hear the roar of the waves and voices of young people
playing croquet. The place was practically cut out of the
solid rock.

The matter which Mr. Frick wanted to see me about
at that time is now well known. Briefly, he made me
custodian of a fund of a quarter of a million dollars the
interest of which is for the betterment of our grade schools
in Pittsburgh, with especial reference to assisting teachers
to improve their methods of teaching. Mr. Frick wished
that the name of the donor of the fund remain unknown,
and it was so for seven years. With his help and consent
I appointed a committee of enthusiastic men to assist in
this important work, but I remained the spokesman of
the unannounced donor. The Educational Fund Commission contained two judges, two experienced members
of local boards of education (now the Board of Public
Education of Pittsburgh), and two manufacturing engineers interested in educational work. At the first meeting of the Commission, October 2, 1909, I was elected
President. We all entered upon our duties with enthusiasm and a deep sense of responsibility which had de-
volved upon us in such an unexpected and unusual
manner.

We recognized that the purely intellectual work of our

schools was well taken care of, but we wanted to find the teacher who had high aims in civic, social health, and manual training lines, those who can and do instill high moral principles as well as have the ability to teach the individual student to think for himself.

I want to quote my friend, Judge Joseph Buffington, one of the original members of the Commission, about the work of the Commission. In announcing the donor and his deed of trust of May 17, 1916, when the annual summer scholarships to the public-school teachers were distributed, he said:

The desire of the donor to now make the fund permanent has necessitated the disclosure of his identity; and at a recent conference with him at which he made the fund of $250,000 permanent, and added an annual income of $12,500 for a term of five years, the donor has at our urgent request permitted us to lift the veil of modest retirement which has hitherto characterized this splendid anonymous gift.

There have been, of course, instances here and there of small gifts to the public schools, but this gift is, historically speaking, I believe, the first and only instance of an endowment by an individual, on a large scale, of an American public-school system.

In starting out on this new field the Commission sought the views of the best educators over the country, but after they had been heard from, the Commission finally, as in most cases of responsibility, had to evolve its own plan. In substance that plan was to create, stimulate, and develop the ambition, field, and vision of the two thousand teachers who were moulding the eighty thousand school children of the city. They determined that in the public school the individual teacher was, in the final analysis, the power behind the gun; and if that teacher could be led from the sphere of humdrum routine into an atmosphere of progressive self-improvement, that the child, the schools, and the community would be benefited.

With that specific end in view — the energizing, vitalizing,

and inspiring the individual teacher — the Commission turned
to the summer schools of pedagogy which were being established
in different parts of the country. These schools were beginning
to draw to their sessions the most ambitious and progressive
teachers, and the Commission determined as an experiment to
select about seventy Pittsburgh teachers and send them to
these schools with the distinct idea of coupling vocational and
vacational work, and enable these teachers to bring back to
Pittsburgh the best ideas they could from the best teachers
from other American cities who attended these summer schools.

It will thus be seen that the basic feature of the Commission
was teaching the child by teaching the teacher, and in doing
that to get the best ideas of the best school work of other cities
and bring that best to the schools of Pittsburgh. . . .

The keynote had been struck, the problem solved. Hence-
forth it was a mere question of going ahead on the lines mapped.
By the time three years had passed, the teachers grasped the
idea of the need of mobilizing the forces and powers which had
been called into being in their summer studies, and the result
was the formation of the Phœbe Brashear Club, a tribute to the
memory of a good woman who had made much of the life-work
of the administrator of this fund possible.

This great club has now, 1917, grown into some seven hundred members.[1] It is the Tenth Legion of the educational
forces of Pittsburgh. It is the dynamic force that inspires the
whole teaching force of the city and reaches the home of every
school child. That great club is divided into some eight different
divisions. . . . It has reached out into the night schools for
foreigners; it has put enthusiasm, sympathy, and energy into
our general night schools where thousands of ambitious people
who work by day, study by night. It has reached out into
settlement work.

Did time allow, much might be said of the many ways in
which the great, silent, purposeful usefulness of this fund is
now working as a vitalizing leaven in the school system of our
city. Dr. William M. Davidson, the efficient head of our schools,
tells me that after an experience in the different great school

---

[1] The eligible beneficiaries of summer scholarships were over fifteen
hundred in 1922.

systems which he served before we were fortunate enough to secure him for Pittsburgh, this educational fund was the strongest and most helpful influence in the practical workings of the school that he found when he came to our city.

He has also stated that in no other place where he had served, had the teaching force aided him in his work as in Pittsburgh.

After long years of educational work, I am convinced that there is no greater field for building up the cardinal principles of our great Republic than the public-school education of our boys and girls, the future hopes of our loved country. Not for a moment do I wish to depreciate the value of the higher institutions of learning, but, when we remember that the number of students in these higher departments of learning are but a small percentage of the teachers and students in our public schools, the relative values of the two can at once be seen.

Associated with the problem of the education of the "rank and file" of our nation, which in my humble opinion can only be solved in the public schools of our country, is the problem of caring for the children of foreign-born parents. Call it Americanization or what you please, it is the problem of building them up into ideal American citizens, instilling into their young minds high principles while giving them the fundamentals of an education. This work we are doing in Pittsburgh with splendid results. We have literally thousands of letters from teachers and students attesting their deep appreciation of the help that has been given them, and some of the finest tributes that have been given come from the various industries employing foreign labor, substantially recognizing the value of our teachers' work among the wives and children of their foreign workmen.

I feel free to say that the splendid gift of Henry Clay
Frick for the betterment of the public schools of Pittsburgh has done more good, more effective work than any
endowment ever given for education, be it in college, university, or public schools. Let us take better care of our
teachers, pay them a living wage, and, my word for it,
the day will come, and that right soon, for it is partly
here already, when our own and the alien will know the
true meaning of liberty, equality, fraternity, love of
country, a love that abideth forever.

CHAPTER XVIII
THIRD TRIP ABROAD

MY third and last trip to Europe was recommended by the Trustees of the University of Pittsburgh. Saint Andrews University of Scotland was to celebrate its five-hundredth anniversary in 1911 and I was requested by the Trustees to go as a delegate of our University. At first I could not see my way clear. My wife had always been my traveling companion, and now that she was gone I was loath to go by myself. But Mr. Carnegie, who had been Lord Rector of Saint Andrews the previous term, had said at one of the meetings of the Board of Trustees of the Carnegie Institute that he and Mrs. Carnegie would gladly welcome any of its members should they visit Skibo at that time, and also pay their expenses.

I concluded it would be a good thing to go for several reasons: first, I should have a chance to meet educators at the great convention from all over the world; second, I should have a chance to visit Skibo; third, I should have the opportunity to make at least a brief visit to friends in Great Britain and France. I should also have an opportunity to run over to Germany for a brief visit. This would give me an opportunity to visit various schools and to come in contact with European educational methods which would prove of advantage to my work as President of the Henry C. Frick Educational Commission, and Mr.

Frick gave me a generous gift of money to be used for that purpose after the Saint Andrews celebration was over.

I secured passage on the Kaiser Wilhelm II, and left home on September 5, 1911. Our ship landed us at Plymouth where I took the special train and went up to London. I did not stay in London any time, but started the same night for Edinburgh. I remember I had breakfast brought to my sleeping apartment the next morning, a practice on the English trains that was certainly a surprise, and very enjoyable. Arriving at Edinburgh, I immediately took train for Saint Andrews, the home of golf and golf links as well as of the old University.

It was impossible to assign all of the many hundreds of delegates from all over the world to quarters in the city, and I was taken care of by Sir Thomas and Lady Gertrude Cochran at Crawford Priory, Springfield, Fifeshire, about fourteen miles from Saint Andrews.

The authorities had erected a temporary building that would hold possibly ten thousand people and it was filled to capacity at some of the meetings. Visitors from Scotland, indeed, from all parts of Great Britain, alumni, old and young, were there in great numbers; and the delegates, as I have already stated, by the hundreds. All delegates were gowned *à la mode* of their own college or university; some of the delegates from India in the most somber hues; some with paraphernalia that, had they by accident been thrown into the water, would have sunk them to the bottom. To my mind the most beautiful garb of all was that of the French delegates who were attired in dress suits with a wide silk scarf thrown over the shoulders, reaching across the breast and fastened in a bow at the side.

The Lord Rector's address was one of the most notable I have ever heard. The whole audience listened with the most profound interest and silence, which was broken once by the hissing of a class of the alumni who did not happen to like the remarks of the speaker. They were almost instantly quieted by their fellow alumni and other classes. After the address was over, the delegates were called to the stage and presented to the audience. Here was an opportunity to see a number of my friends, who were delegates from America and whom I should not have known were there except for an occasion like this. Among them were Dr. Smith, Provost of the University of Pennsylvania, and Dr. Peterson, of McGill University, who had at one time been connected with Saint Andrews. I also met Mr. and Mrs. Carnegie who left for Skibo before the close of the meeting, but not before they had made arrangements for me to come to visit them. They advised me to stop over at Inverness for a night and leave the next day for Bonar Bridge, the station nearest Skibo, where they would meet me and take me to their home.

One of the last days of the Saint Andrews celebration was devoted to a meeting in Dundee where a branch of the University had been established. The meeting was very interesting, but after luncheon I decided to leave and visit Broughty Ferry, not very far distant, the home of Dr. Thomas Dick, author of Dick's "Works," which my grandfather had owned and given to me in my boyhood. What reverent joy was mine that afternoon as I paid homage to the memory of the dear man who had done so much to rouse my interest in the science of astronomy in my early youth!

I left Crawford Priory with many pleasant memories of the dear people there, and took a train to Inverness where I arrived late in the evening. I had little opportunity to see the city that night, but I was up early the next morning and tramped to some of the most interesting spots before taking my train for Bonar Bridge. In the train were several persons who seemed to be well acquainted with one another; of course, I knew none of them. When we reached Bonar Bridge Station there was an omnibus and an automobile waiting for us, and when we reached the castle, Mr. and Mrs. Carnegie met us at the entrance. I was very much surprised to find that among my fellow passengers were David Lloyd George and his associate, the Master of Elybanks, who was called the "whip" of the Liberal Party. The editor of the London "Spectator" and his wife and daughter were also among the guests who came with us. We reached the Castle a short time before lunch. That lunch was a memorable one for me because of the privilege of meeting so many eminent people. I learned a little later that the reason for the visit of Lloyd George, the Master of Elybanks, and the editor of the London "Spectator" was to be with Mr. Carnegie to receive the news of the results of the election in Canada, as one of the main objects of the Liberal Party of Canada was to try to win out for reciprocity. Unfortunately for our host and his friends, the results were against their wishes, and it was not difficult to understand their disappointment. The spirit of brotherhood is now between us, however, as no mere election could ever have made it.

The first afternoon at Skibo was spent taking walks through the beautiful gardens and grounds surrounding the Castle. In the course of the afternoon Mr. Carnegie asked me if I would give them a talk on astronomy that evening. Mrs. Carnegie had some beautiful transparencies, copies of photographs taken by the sixty-inch telescope at Mount Wilson, so arranged that they could be illuminated from the rear. An examination of the pictures at once told me they were all familiar objects in the heavens. That evening and the next two evenings I had the pleasure of giving a talk on my hobby in one of the lovely rooms at Skibo with an audience composed of such people as I have already noted, and the family and friends who gathered each evening. For a year afterward I would occasionally receive a copy of the "Druid," a paper devoted to the interests of the Welsh people in America, in which there would be an account of a lecture by Lloyd George, possibly for the benefit of some Baptist institution, in which he would mention matters of which he had heard me speak at those evening meetings at Skibo. Since then this splendid man has done memorable work during and after the war, but mention of his name brings first to my mind the kindly friendship he gave me while we were at Skibo together.

During my visit I went with Mr. and Mrs. Carnegie to the public school in which they took great interest, Mrs. Carnegie awarding a number of prizes at the time. Another interesting incident was a trip that Mr. Carnegie, George Lauder, and I made on the good steamer Sea

Breeze. After passing a nest of English battleships we
sat down to a little lunch, and then Mr. Lauder and Mr.
Carnegie fixed themselves comfortably under the canvas
and went to sleep; so I was the sole passenger awake. I
soon made acquaintance with the captain who proved a
communicative soul. We sailed past the old castle which
was at one time used for the storing of wines smuggled
from France; but the most interesting place of all that
we passed on that pleasant trip was the cliffs of red sand-
stone made memorable by Hugh Miller in his geological
studies. At one place we passed a cave where the captain
told me Miller was once studying inside when the tide
rose so high he could not get out again until the tide re-
ceded. We went as far as a bay where we found more
British greyhounds before returning home.

On Sunday Mr. and Mrs. Carnegie and their daughter
Margaret made a tour of the workmen's homes distributing presents among the children. On Sunday evening
there was a song service in the big hallway of the Castle,
Mrs. Carnegie presiding at the organ. The workmen,
their wives and families, were invited, and I heard some
very good music sung by these people. Every morning
the guests and the family were awakened at seven-thirty
by the music of the bagpipes, as the piper walked around
the Castle; and so far as I can remember, every morning
except one the tune was the same. I confess that I have
never yet learned to have a very great affection for the
music of bagpipes. I think this is almost entirely due to
the fact that the bass parts, which I believe are called
drones, are not in harmony with the melody. However,
the enthusiasm of the piper usually makes up for a large

part of this deficiency. In the evening the piper led the procession to dinner, marched entirely around the table, and then walked off to the side of the room until the guests were all seated, when he retired.

My stay at Skibo was certainly one of great pleasure. The heather on the mountain-side was too far gone to be seen in its greatest beauty; nevertheless, the tint was still there, and I could imagine what the mountain had looked like at its best. Upon leaving Skibo I stopped at Dunfermline at Mr. Carnegie's request to study the technical schools there, with particular reference to the linen industries. He gave me a letter of introduction to the head of the various institutions there, and I was shown every courtesy and learned a lot of things of interest in my own educational work. From there I went direct to the Girls' Agricultural School at Studley Castle, presided over by Dr. Lillias Hamilton whom I had met while at Crawford Priory.

I have never seen a more devoted set of teachers and students in the particular studies applicable to agriculture than I found at this wonderful school. I understand it was started by Lady Warwick; and as it became too big an undertaking for her, Dr. Lillias Hamilton took charge of it on her return from South Africa. The young women of this college would take their lessons in the morning and then go into the fields, gardens, and conservatories; and although a large percentage of them were daughters of well-to-do lawyers, merchants, ministers, etc., they were fitting themselves for vocations which would be profitable and pleasant as well. Their work in the conservatories particularly interested me. Such

grapes I had never seen; and in quite a large number of
houses they were raised under glass. I was told that no
less than three crops were raised each year, all of which
found a ready market in London and other places, except
what was used in the institution itself. I saw those young
women by the score in calico dresses and aprons kneeling
down and plucking the weeds out of the beds, and though
it was a rainy day, they were working away, minding it as
little as old farmers.

I was shown a model dairy, operated by the faculty
and students, the like of which I have never seen in any
of my travels. I would like to say more about this model
institution. There is a need of just such an institution as
this in our own country; indeed, in all countries.

While in Leeds I had an opportunity to study the
woolen industries, with particular reference to the technical schools connected with them. Here I found that
the young men and women were educated in every branch
of the industry. They were taught not only to make
drawings of the intricate patterns and figures woven into
the woolen goods, but also to make the cards for the Jac-
quard looms — probably the most wonderful invention
in the woolen and linen industries; for here the figures
and designs are worked in the cards that regulate the
shuttles in the looms, to do what might well be illustrated
by the perforated rolls of the piano-player. In my later
visit to China and Japan I noticed that all the designs
and figures worked in the silks of these two great silk-
producing countries were produced by the laborious hand-
shifting of the shuttles.

I had a delightful visit with a number of friends in

London, among them Sir James and Lady Dewar, and
Mr. Maw. I ran up to Cambridge to pay a brief visit to
Mr. and Mrs. Newall, and Sir Robert and Lady Ball.
While in London I called at the home of Madeline Pitt-
Taylor and her father and mother. I had made what
proved to be a lasting friendship with Madeline Pitt-
Taylor and her aunt, Louise Pitt-Taylor, during the time
of their visit as special guests of Pittsburgh during our
Sesqui-Centennial Celebration. Madeline had been a
visitor to our Observatory and had taken great interest
in our work, and we had since then kept up a correspondence. I was received very kindly by them at tea
one afternoon, and was invited to dine with them the
next evening. That morning I found I had taken a
severe cold, called by the British people "influenza"; and
by afternoon I became so ill that I had to go to bed. I
sent word that it would be impossible for me to come to
them, and the next morning Madeline and her father
were at the hotel early to look after my comfort. Fortunately there was a good doctor from some place in the
southland who was there to study the disease of pellagra.
I remember that the next night I was so ill that I asked
the room-maid to bring me a card on which I wrote the
address of Mr. Carnegie and Sir James Dewar, so that
they could be communicated with if anything happened
to me. However, in a few days I began to feel like myself,
and made a few calls before I left for France.

I reached Paris in time for an interesting affair which
I shall always remember with pleasure. Baron Destournelles de Constant, who had been in this country studying American problems and had given a beautiful talk

at Carnegie Institute, learned that I was coming to Paris and sent me an invitation to the wedding of his son, which awaited me at the Hôtel de Lille et d'Albion. The wedding was to take place in a church the afternoon following my arrival in Paris. I asked an English lady who was stopping at the hotel and who seemed to be acquainted with French customs how I should dress for the occasion. She informed me that I should go in a full-dress suit, as Destournelles was not only a Baron but a Senator. I, therefore, put on my best, went to the church with my invitation, and when the gendarme asked me for my card and saw that it was a special invitation from the Baron, I was taken to one of the best seats in the church. Strange to say, all the gentlemen had come in their afternoon attire, just as if they had come from their places of business, and I found later on that I was the only one who wore a dress-suit. I felt out of place, but nevertheless did the honors the best I could. There were two short sermons before the ceremony, and some beautiful music. The ceremony was simple and very beautiful. After it was over, the audience followed the bride and groom, the attendants and the family, into the minister's study. I lingered until the last, and, giving my name to the gentleman who was introducing along the line, I shook hands and congratulated the bridal party. Just as I reached the end of the line, there was my dear friend the Baron. He gave me a most cordial greeting, took me back to the other end of the line again and introduced me as his friend from America, to the bride, the groom, his wife, and the relatives in attendance. He then instructed his secretary to place me in a carriage with some of the members of the family. I went to the house with them and had a delightful tea, being introduced to many persons who were friends of the Baron and his family.

From Paris I went to Belgium, where I had a conference with the Director of the Observatory located at Uccle, just a few miles from Brussels. We had constructed an astronomical photographic camera for this Observatory, and the Director wanted some changes made in it. From Brussels I went direct to Munich. My purpose was to study the technical schools of that city with a thoroughness for which I had had no opportunity in Great Britain and France. Dr. Kirschensteiner had visited America and had given some illustrated lectures on the technical schools of Munich. I went to New York to listen to one of these lectures and was so much impressed with it that I told Mr. Frick that I would like to visit Munich to study their technical schools, particularly their compulsory trade schools.

Of course I went to see Dr. Kirschensteiner first, and he gave me a letter of introduction to several principals whom I visited from day to day. I saw many things that I thought could well be introduced into the schools of America; but there were some things that did not impress me as of value. The general idea was to take all young men up to eighteen years of age from their places of employment to study ten hours in the technical schools, one day every week. I visited compulsory schools where they taught many vocations, some with the aid of rather crude apparatus, which, they explained, was because many of the young men would have to go into the country later on and work with the tools and apparatus which were there available. For instance, in a blacksmith shop I found boys working the bellows to heat the fire for the smith, although they had a fan for the purpose in the shop, for many of them would go to shops where only man-power would be available.

After my visit to the schools for young men, I went to Dr. Kirschensteiner to ask for a card of admission to the school for young women, and I was surprised to learn that they had no free vocational schools for young women. But he gave me a letter to Baroness von Horn, who had a fine private school that the city helped by a small donation each year.

My friend Charlie Leisser went with me on my first visit to Baroness von Horn's school. I found her a most interesting lady, deeply imbued with the spirit of educating the young working-women of Munich. I was taken by her to the top floor of the building — no elevator to carry me there — where I found a typical laundry. I thought it rather queer to have a laundry on the top floor, but she gave very excellent reasons for placing it there, among them that the vapor of the drying clothes would not have to pass up through the rooms below. As there was to be a lecture in German to some young women who were studying household economy (which Booker Washington told me was called "cooking" at Tuskegee), I went with the Baroness to the basement and listened to a description of how to cook a kidney. Although the lecture was in German I could understand it fairly well, and as the lecturer talked, a servant brought models of various kinds of fungi — among them, of course, the edible mushroom — such as are used for garnishing a dish of kidneys. I thoroughly enjoyed listening to the queries of the students, showing their interest in the various steps of making this dish palatable and nutritious. Later on, during my second visit, I was informed by Baroness von Horn that the city gave her only four hundred marks to help her in her work; but each day from one hundred and fifty to two hundred lunches were sold to clerks, storekeepers, and others in the vicinity of the school, which helped them to bear the expenses.

After my stay in Munich I started north for Jena where the firm of Schott and Company had made the optical disks for the thirty-inch telescope for the Allegheny Observatory. They had delivered the crown, and the flint was ready for delivery in case it satisfied me. Everything had been arranged for my study of the glass, and I had the pleasure of examining what proved to be, in all likelihood, one of the best pieces of flint glass that had ever been made for a large telescope objective.

Contrary to my expectations I was taken through the factories of the Schott and Company establishment. They had started on a very small scale ten years before my visit, and Dr. Schott informed me that their output was about one hundred kilograms of optical glass the first year. The year I was there they expected to produce not less than one hundred and twenty thousand kilograms.

The two disks for the thirty-inch refractor of the Allegheny Observatory, the curves of which were calculated by Dr. Hastings, and ground, polished, and figured by Mr. McDowell, have made one of the most efficient instruments in the world, not alone on account of its accurate figuring, but on account of the great transparency of the glass made by this firm. Later on, they made for us the twenty-inch disk for the objective of the Oakland (California) Observatory, which, after being tested by Dr. Aitken of the Lick Observatory, has satisfied the most exact requirements of a glass of that size. During my stay in Jena I took many walks up the hillside, where I could look over the red-tile roofs that were characteristic of that city.

After a short visit with some relatives near Hanover, I left for Bremen, where I at once took passage for the land I loved best of all. I believe it is the custom of all passenger steamships to have a concert or some entertainment for the benefit of the sailors' widows and orphans. On this occasion the captain requested me to be chairman of the entertainment committee. Caruso was on board on his way to America to sing at the Metropolitan Opera House; but he refused to help us, claiming that he had agreed with the Metropolitan people not to sing for any one but them. We succeeded in gathering a coterie of singers and players, among them a young fellow not over fifteen years of age who was really a freak at the piano. During the intermission I made a plea for the fund for the widows and orphans. The result of the appeal was very nearly seven hundred dollars, which was said to be quite phenomenal and gratifying to all.

We reached the harbor of New York, to me the City Beautiful; and soon I was back in dear old Pittsburgh.

APPENDIX
PART I

LANGLEY'S AUTOGRAPH ORDER FOR AN
AIRPLANE MODEL

ALLEGHENY, *March* 8, '87

DEAR MR. BRASHEAR,

Here is a rough sketch of the model I described in detail yesterday and of which I want material for 3 copies. To recapitulate essentials. a_1 a_2 a_1 a_2 are two hollow brass rods 100 centimetres long 2.5 @ 3 cm. diameter. They are very light and hold within long twisted rubber springs which act by their torsion on the wheels. *p.p.* is the supporting plane, strengthened on the front by a rib, held by sliding collars which move along the rods and with an angle adjustable on these collars. The point of support is 1/3 the depth of plane from front. The wheels carry four vanes. *S.s.s.S.* length of each vane 15 cm. width at broadest 5 cm. A stiffening wire runs outside. Angle of vanes adjustable. r is the rudder shaped like the tail of a child's dart. + It is revolvable on the light central rod *d.d.* and had better if possible be adjustable in 3 ps. above or below this rod as well as concentric with it. As shown in fig. 4 the end of each axle should project with a square head to admit of the rubber spring being wound up by a key also. (Fig. 1) there should be a trigger t t to release the wound-up wheels by.

As to Weight, Area, Power and Speed.

Weight of whole is limited, to *about* One Kilogramme, or to 1. gramme. to every $2^\square$ centimetres of sustaining plane surface. It is supposed that we can store up 500 turns of the rubber in each rod representing in English measure about 500 ft. pounds each. This may take about 1/3 pd. rubber each. The *maximum* pitch of the wheels will be an angle of 45° giving probably (allow-ing for slip) about 50 cm. advance for each turn. i.e. 20 turns per second then will give, on this (assumption) about 20 miles an hour.

The whole is to be constructed with a constant eye to future modifications. That arrangement will be best which allows size of planes-vanes etc. to be altered after trial. If light brass tubing can be found in stock enough for several models should be ordered.

S. P. LANGLEY

PART II

SOME ideas of Dr. Brashear's contribution to modern science may be obtained from a partial list of some of the important instruments, apparatus, and lenses which were completed in his shops.

The spectroscope for the Lick Observatory, completed about 1888. James E. Keeler, then at Lick Observatory, made with this instrument his now classic visual studies of the motion of the nebulæ in the line of sight, with a mean error of 3.2 kilometers per second.

The spectroscope for the Halstead Observatory used by C. A. Young chiefly in investigating solar spectra. With this instrument Young observed in 1892 many double lines in the spectra of sun-spots, then supposed to be the effect of "reversal" by superposed gaseous layers at different temperatures, but subsequently shown to be caused by magnetic fields.

Special apparatus for Professor Comstock which enabled him to determine the constant of refraction, by comparing stars at great distances apart.

Optical surfaces for Professor A. A. Michelson's first interferometer; and subsequently the optical train for the International Bureau of Paris, to measure the value of the meter in terms of a wave-length of light.

The first spectroheliograph to photograph automatically the surface and surroundings of the sun, made for Dr. George E. Hale. Its results have been epoch-making in the realm of solar photography.

A spectroscope for Professor Keeler, who had become Director of the old Allegheny Observatory, and wished to continue his photographic study of the motion of nebulæ, stars, and planets in the line of sight. His work was very successful, culminating in his beautiful demonstration of the meteoritic character of Saturn's rings. This instrument has a flat Rowland Grating 1.3 inches by 1.8 inches, with 14,438 ruled lines to the inch; and also a train of three prisms of dense flint glass.

The Mills's spectrograph, completed in 1894, for Director W. W. Campbell, of the Lick Observatory, who used it in his extensive stellar spectroscopic investigations, which yielded among other results the velocity at which the sun, earth, and other planets are moving toward the constellation of the Lyre.

It is doubtful whether any other stellar spectrograph ever contained prisms more perfect than those made by Brashear for this instrument. The thousands of sharply defined photographs of stellar spectra obtained with it by Dr. Campbell and his colleagues rendered possible a new and revolutionary attack on the motions of the stars, which has yielded conclusions of the widest significance.

A large star spectroscope for the forty-inch refractor of the Yerkes Observatory, to detect motions of stars and nebulæ in the line of sight.

A star spectroscope for the United States Naval Observatory; optical equipment of the Bruce Spectrograph for the University of Cambridge, England, and for the Cape of Good Hope star-spectroscope.

Large universal spectroscopes were supplied to many other observatories, one of the best being that of the Lowell Observatory in Arizona.

Mention has been made of the first manufacture of Rowland Gratings on the Brashear plates. It may be interesting to note that in the decade following 1890, some of the largest-size concave-grating spectroscopes were supplied to:

West Point Military Academy.
Sloane Physical Laboratory.
Royal University of Ireland (Trinity), Dublin.
Cambridge University, England.
University of Turin, Italy.
Dr. Houswaldt's Physical Laboratory, Magdeburg, Germany.
McGill University, Montreal.
Paris Observatory, Paris, France.

Perhaps nothing better reveals the growth of the Brashear Works than a list of some of the larger telescope objectives and mirrors completed subsequent to 1888.

12-inch object glass — Syrian Protestant College, Beirut, Syria.
12-inch object glass — University of Illinois, Champaign, Illinois.
12-inch object glass — Ohio State University, Columbus, Ohio.
Two 12-inch object glasses for Kenwood Observatory, Chicago.
12-inch object glass for Dudley Observatory, Albany.
12-inch object glass, 150 feet focal length, for Mount Wilson Tower Telescope.

12-inch object glass for Ladd Observatory, Providence, Rhode Island.

15-inch object glass — Yale University, New Haven, Connecticut.

14-inch object glass — Philadelphia High School, Philadelphia, Pennsylvania.

16-inch object glass for Carleton College Observatory, Northfield, Minnesota.

15-inch object glass for S. N. Smith's Private Observatory, Newport News, Virginia.

15-inch object glass — Dominion Astronomical Observatory, Ottawa, Canada.

18-inch object glass for Flower Observatory, University of Pennsylvania, Philadelphia, Pennsylvania.

15-inch object glass for Philadelphia High School.

12-inch object glass for University of Indiana, Bloomington, Indiana.

30-inch reflector for the Keeler Memorial — Allegheny Observatory, Pittsburgh, Pennsylvania.

30-inch plane mirror — Yale University, New Haven, Connecticut.

37-inch Cassegrain telescope for Professor Campbell's expedition to Chile in connection with the Lick researches on the motion of the stars in the line of sight.

37-inch parabolic mirror — University of Michigan, Ann Arbor, Michigan.

19½-inch plane and parabolic mirrors — Dominion Observatory, Victoria, Canada.

20-inch object glass — Chabot Observatory, Oakland, California.

24-inch object glass — Swarthmore College, Swarthmore, Pennsylvania.

The thirty-inch object glass of the great Thaw Memorial Telescope, built by the Brashear Company with especial reference to photographic work, is, for such purpose, more powerful than larger visual instruments, and is rendering noteworthy service in systematic stellar photography by a rapid and accurate method developed at the Allegheny Observatory.

The history of this large refracting telescope, a triumph of the optical-instrument maker's art and science, reveals some of the causes of their great cost, and of the time required to make them. Owing to the extreme difficulty of obtaining glass disks of the requisite size, free from striæ, from inequalities in the density specified, from hygroscopic and other defects — some of which are only discovered after the glass has been polished — the length of time required to complete them cannot be foreseen. In this case the Brashear Company was able to obtain satisfactory disks only after a period of seventeen years subsequent to placing the first order in Europe.

Among the successful instruments of the Brashear Company, involving its best theoretical and practical resources, are its photographic doublets, whose lenses are constructed according to an original solution of Dr. Charles S. Hastings, which gives a large and flat photographic field of the sky.

They have been sent to various parts of the world and have been instrumental in making numerous discoveries. Dr. Max Wolf, of the University of Heidelberg, has been particularly successful in discovering new asteroids with his sixteen-inch doublet, capturing on one night alone five strangers on each of his two plates. Two cameras are used so that the trails of the asteroids, which are apt to resemble a defect on the photographic plate, may be readily identified by their same relative position among the stars on the two plates. Dr. Wolf has shown his appreciation of his success with this sixteen-inch Brashear doublet by naming two of the many planetoids discovered with it "Alleghenia" and "Pittsburghia," the latter estimated to be about 260,000,000 miles from the earth.

In October, 1913, the Brashear Company was awarded by the Canadian Government the contract for the optical parts of a seventy-two-inch reflecting telescope for the Dominion Observatory at Victoria, British Columbia, the mechanical parts being awarded to the Warner & Swasey Company, of Cleveland. Dr. Brashear was then completing his seventy-third year, with public duties sufficient to occupy all the working hours of younger men. But he entered upon this, his last great optical task — the world's second largest telescope, only exceeded by the Mount Wilson one-hundred-inch reflector — with as great enthusiasm as he had shown in his youth, when after long hours in the rolling-mill he ground and polished his first five-inch lens which he was too poor to buy.

PART III

THE following lists, long, though incomplete, of Brashear's honors, memberships, and degrees, show his wide activities and recognitions, so many of which he modestly fails to mention in his Autobiography.

HONORS

1884. Medal of Award, Massachusetts Charitable Mechanic Association.

1889. President of Engineers' Society of Western Pennsylvania.

1890–1892. Vice-President, Academy of Science and Art, Pittsburgh.

1892–1896. President, Academy of Science and Art, Pittsburgh.

1894–1920. Chairman of Allegheny Observatory Committee of the University of Pittsburgh.

1896–1920. Member of Board of Trustees of Carnegie Institute.

1896–1920. Member of Board of Trustees of University of Pittsburgh.

1898–1900. Acting Director of Allegheny Observatory.

1900. Vice-President of American Association for the Advancement of Science, Section D.

1900. Medal, Exposition Universelle Internationale, République Française.

1901. Member of Committee on Plan and Scope of Carnegie Institute during the planning and erection of the Technical Schools, and actively connected with its successor, the Committee on Institute of Technology, until his death.

1901. Member of Assay Commission, appointed by President of United States.

1901–1904. Acting Chancellor of Western University of Pennsylvania.

1903. President of Crucible Club.

1903. As a tribute to Dr. Brashear, because he had made the glass with which new asteroids had been discovered, Dr. Max Wolf, Director of Heidelberg Observatory, asked him to name one of them. He called it "Pittsburghia."

187

1904. "Grand Prize" at St. Louis Exposition.

1909. Member of Langley Gold Medal Commission, appointed by Regents of Smithsonian Institution.

1909–1920. Chairman of Educational Fund Commission, afterwards known as Henry C. Frick Educational Commission.

1910. Elliott Cresson Gold Medal from Franklin Institute.

1910–1920. Member of Board of Corporators of Western Pennsylvania School for the Blind.

1911. Delegate from University of Pittsburgh to the 500th Anniversary Celebration at University of Saint Andrews, Scotland.

1911–1916. Member of John Fritz Medal Board of Award.

1915. President of The American Society of Mechanical Engineers.

1915. Delegate from A.S.M.E. to the International Engineers Congress.

1915. United States delegate to Second Pan-American Scientific Congress, appointed by Secretary of State Lansing.

1915. Appointment by Governor Brumbaugh, of Pennsylvania, as Pennsylvania's "most distinguished citizen," and celebration of "Brashear Day" in connection with the Panama-Pacific International Exposition at San Francisco.

"Medal of Award" for exhibit of scientific instruments at Panama-Pacific Exposition.

1917. Member of Executive Committee of Joseph A. Holmes Safety Association.

1918. Member of National Research Council.

HONORARY DEGREES

1893. Western University of Pennsylvania, now University of Pittsburgh, Sc.D.

1896. University of Wooster, LL.D.

1902. Washington and Jefferson College, LL.D.

1911. Princeton University, Sc.D.

1912. Stevens Institute of Technology, D.Eng.

1916. University of Pittsburgh, LL.D.

Art Society of Pittsburgh.

Fellow of American Association for the Advancement of Science; Life Member in 1902.

Civic Club of Allegheny County.

British Westinghouse Club.

Engineers Society of Western Pennsylvania.

Engineers Club of New York.

Duquesne Club, Pittsburgh.

Pittsburgh Athletic Association.

Junta Club, Pittsburgh.

University Club, Washington, D.C.

American Society of Mechanical Engineers.

Royal Astronomical Society of Canada.

Aero Club of America.

Phi Zeta Phi, later Phi Gamma Delta, at University of Pittsburgh.

Fellows Club, Pittsburgh.

"?" Club (Quiz Club), Pittsburgh (first Honorary Member).

Phœbe Brashear Club of Pittsburgh.

California Academy of Sciences.

Chamber of Commerce, Pittsburgh (Andrew Carnegie and Dr. Brashear were the only Honorary Members of this organization to date).

Franklin Institute.

Honorary Member of Local Alumni Association of:

  University of Illinois.

  Purdue University.

  Carnegie Institute of Technology.

  Tufts College.

  Kenyon College.

  Johns Hopkins University.

  Cornell University.

  Haverford College.

  University of Michigan.

  University of Wisconsin.

  University of Pennsylvania.

  Centre College.

  Harvard University.

  Columbia University.

  Lehigh University.

MEMBERSHIPS

Franklin Literary Society, South Side, Pittsburgh.
Art Society of Pittsburgh.
Guyasuta Lodge, No. 513, Free and Accepted Masons.
Andrew Carnegie's Naturalist's Club, Carnegie Museum.
Historical Society of Western Pennsylvania.
Academy of Science and Art, Pittsburgh, Pennsylvania (charter
    member).
American Astronomical Society.
Pittsburgh Aquarium Society.
Audubon Society of Western Pennsylvania.
Société Astronomique de France.
Astronomical Society of the Pacific.
British Astronomical Association.
Société Belge d'Astronomie.
Fellow of Royal Astronomical Society (London).
Fellow of American Philosophical Society.
International Congress on "Photographie Céleste."
Kenyon Club, Pittsburgh.
Hungry Club of Pittsburgh.
Pennsylvania Society of New York.
Hospital School for Backward Children Association, Pittsburgh.
Cosmos Club, Washington, D.C.
Author's Club, Pittsburgh.
Montessori Educational Association, Washington, D.C.
Washington Academy of Sciences.
National Research Council, Engineering Section.
Boy and Girl Scouts, and Camp Fire Girls of Allegheny County.